S0-EDI-434

THE MANLY HANDBOOK

THE MANLY HANDBOOK

DAVID EVERITT and HAROLD SCHECHTER

BERKLEY BOOKS, NEW YORK

A manly tip of the hat to all the guys who helped with ideas and material for this book: Bob Hughes, David Sherman, Bruce Epstein, Stan Willard, Richard Schotter, Bruce Santner, Bill Kelly, and the boys at Jerry Ohlinger's. Also, we'd like to pay tribute to those immortal men who have been such an inspiration to us throughout our lives, namely General William Tecumseh Sherman, Douglas MacArthur, and Ernest Borgnine.

THE MANLY HANDBOOK

A Berkley Book / published by arrangement with the authors

PRINTING HISTORY
Berkley trade paperback edition / July 1982

For information address: Berkley Publishing Corporation, 200 Madison Avenue, New York, New York 10016.

ISBN: 0-425-05647-3

A BERKLEY BOOK® TM 757,375
The name "BERKLEY" and the stylized "B" with design are trademarks belonging to Berkley Publishing Corporation.
PRINTED IN THE UNITED STATES OF AMERICA.

CONTENTS

NAME: Mickey Spillane
OCCUPATION: Man

PREFACE

YOU, TOO, CAN BE A MAN

What, another "handbook"? Guess again, soldier. The volume you now hold in your hands is not only unique but indispensable to the very survival of our country as we know it. What makes this handy reference work so special? Walk into any bookstore these days and you'll find the shelves crammed with guides, manuals, and how-to volumes on every conceivable subject: how to grow organic vegetables, how to care for your cat, how to breast-feed your baby, how to save your marriage, how to slim your hips, how to enjoy sex, how to be a preppie. Notice anything funny? No? Well, put it this way: try to imagine John Wayne reading a book on organic gardening or cat care. (Of course, the Duke hasn't been doing any reading at all for the past few years; but use your imagination.) Get the picture? Every other how-to book is written for *women. The Manly Handbook,* on the other hand, is the only manly book of its kind on the marketplace—an essential guide for anyone who wants to be a man.

In a society in which the very concept of manliness is being everywhere undermined by insidious social movements, we feel that it's high time somebody stepped forward with a book that speaks directly to the needs of men, the sort of book a real man can enjoy—one that is straight-shooting, square-dealing, and doesn't use a lot of big words. With the appearance of *The Manly Handbook* there is hope at last for all those millions of people yearning to know, in this age of runaway feminization, how they, too, can be truly manly. And by purchasing this book, you won't just be doing yourself a favor. More important, you'll be helping to keep America strong. If you read only one book this year (and since reading isn't very manly, you'll want to hold yourself to that limit), remember: this is the one the Duke would have wanted you to buy.

Maybe you're still asking yourself: Is this the right book for me? Or, more accurately: Am I the right person for this book? Do I have what it takes to handle this kind of reading experience? Do I have the guts, the balls, the right stuff—and, most critical of all, the $3.95? To help determine whether you are qualified or not, we have provided the following, easy-to-understand checklist.

If you

☐ **Don't wear designer jeans**

☐ **Stay up till all hours of the morning to watch reruns of any TV program starring Robert Conrad**

☐ **Instantly switch stations when a Barry Manilow song comes on the radio**

☐ **Daydream about leading a terrorist attack against the "Richard Simmons Show"**

☐ **Aren't French**

...Then you, too, can be manly!

PART ONE

THE COMPLEAT MAN

WHAT IS A MAN?

It is a sad commentary on the age we live in that we find it necessary to begin our book with a brief description of true manliness. But recent lamentable developments in this once manly nation of ours make a definition of this kind unavoidable.

To begin with, man is the opposite of woman. If you have any intention of being a woman in any respect, then manliness is not for you. Either you are a man or a woman. The choice is yours.

Once this central, though increasingly overlooked, concept is grasped, we can move on to a more subtle distinction, one that has escaped too many people for too long. After glancing at the contents of this book, some careless readers may respond by saying, "Oh, this is just some *macho* thing, right?"

Wrong.

There is a world of difference between manly and *macho*. If you're looking for a guidebook that will tell you what gold necklace to wear with which kind of shirt opened down to the navel, then you're barking up the wrong tree, buckaroo. What, we ask, does wearing a necklace have to do with being a man? And if you're interested

The choice is yours: Do you want to be a man . . . or a woman?

in obtaining advice on what so-called men's cologne (a contradiction in terms if ever there was one) to choose for a night out on the town, then you are similarly misguided. A man doesn't wear cologne. He wears sweat. *Macho* should in no way be mistaken for manly. *Macho* is a woman's word popularized by New York City's *Village Voice* to describe anyone who doesn't read poetry and cry. The qualifications for manliness are far more rigorous.

Simply stated—the essence of manliness is comportment. To be a man, one must comport oneself in a manly manner in every area of one's life. When waking up in the morning, when going to work, when relaxing in the evening, when hitting the sack—one must comport oneself at all times and never stop comporting. In a word, comportment is all. The business of *The Manly Handbook* is to define exactly what comportment entails.

One last, vital point before we move on to the specifics, to the nuts and bolts of becoming a man. We want to stress that we are not dealing with some kind of elitist clique or exclusive club in this book. Elitism goes against the grain of every true American; check out any history book, and you'll find that the whole idea of elitism started with the commies. Manliness is an equal opportunity enterprise. Regardless of your background or your present unmanly situation in life, you still may cross over to the manly style. We don't care what political party you once belonged to or what so-called "health club" or "bathhouse" you used to be a member of; from here on in, the slate is wiped clean. As we will demonstrate over and over again, anyone can be a man (except for those people who insist on being women). All that is required in the individual is a burning desire to comport. Remember: Manhood belongs to the world. Provided, of course, that you're an American.

COMPORT THYSELF: THE FIRST COMMANDMENT OF MANLINESS

Before the beginner can embark on his lifelong mission of manliness, he must first familiarize himself with the fundamental principles of manly comportment. Once these have been fully absorbed, they will enable the aspiring man to lead a life of total gusto. Without these basics, he may as well quit his job and become a hairdresser.

First, let us review the recent, deplorable social developments that have made a guide to manliness such a vital necessity. In the past twenty years, largely as the result of certain unfortunate loopholes in the U.S. Constitution (such as the First Amendment), every crackpot minority group imaginable has started some kind of movement. The first of these to make its noxious influence felt was the so-called peace movement of the 1960s. Striking the first blow against manliness, these gutless commie sympathizers maintained that we should turn tail and run in Vietnam just when things were starting to get interesting. Simultaneously, and often overlapping with the peace weirdos, were the sex-and-drug-crazed hippies, who went around preaching that men should wear long hair and beaded necklaces, act in a gentle and passive manner, and take an unnatural, not to say completely un-American, interest in love. (Note: Any real man reading this capsule history may already find himself becoming apoplectic with rage. If so, we suggest that you take a little break—have a couple of drinks, go out and change the oil in your car—till the feeling blows over.)

By the early seventies, the hippies were, happily, dwindling in numbers. But the crisis was far from over. From out of nowhere, the Feminist Movement came along to inform us that women (get this) were just as good as men. Then, even while the country was still reeling from the hysterical assaults of these vicious lesbian propagandists, we were suddenly hit by the Gay Movement. In the interest of manly sensibilities everywhere, we feel that the less said about this subject the better.

When you consider what kind of impact each of these fanatical pro-commie movements has had on the social fabric of this once great nation of ours, the urgency of our present situation becomes clear. Left unchecked, these virulently anti-manly groups threaten to turn America into a nation of disco roller skaters.

Fortunately, the tide can still be turned. Everyone has had his—excuse us, we mean *her*—little say: the fifth-columnist pinkos, the love sickos, the skirts, the queers, the lesbians, the fairies—even the homosexuals. Fair enough. This is America. We believe in freedom of speech, even when the people speaking are the lowest kind of parasites and traitors who should be locked away for the rest of their worthless lives or sent back to the Ukraine where they belong. But now it's time to fight back. Manliness—that sacred quality that is the very foundation of our American democratic system of government—is under heavy assault from an army of left-wing, feminizing forces that will stop at nothing to turn the Pentagon into a giant day-care center. But that's okay. A real man *likes* to be assaulted. In fact, it's one of the ways you can tell a man from a woman. A real man *welcomes* assault, particularly with a deadly weapon, because it gives him a chance to show that he can take it like a man.

As this bleak yet depressing look at recent events in our cultural history shows, anyone inquiring into the essentials of

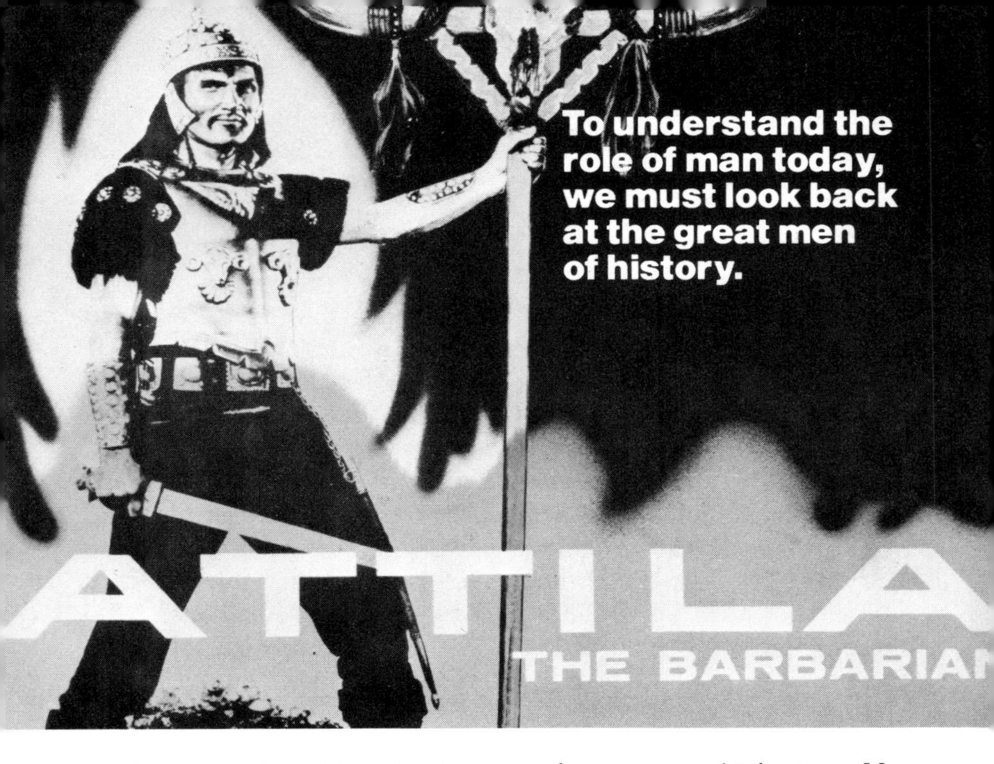

manly comportment is going to be deeply disappointed if he restricts himself to the last twenty years. To understand the true nature of manliness, we must turn back to the very beginning of life on earth.

Man was put on this planet for one purpose and one purpose only: to act like a man. Imagine, for a moment, the Garden of Eden. God needed someone to get the human race going, so what did He do? Did He send down a modern dancer? No way. He sent down someone He could count on, someone who could hack it, someone who wouldn't choke under pressure. At the time, He couldn't afford to call in Pete Rose (He had other plans for him in the late innings), so He sent along Adam to pinch-hit. As it turned out, this might not have been the best choice, but that's not the Manager's fault. How was He to know that Adam would go all sappy over some dame and violate one of the basic principles of manly comportment? The hard fact is that manliness carries certain obligations with it; it isn't something that is bestowed on us for free. The Big Fella up in the clouds is no communist. We must earn our manliness by doing manly works, which is the essence of comportment. God, in short, doesn't like pantywaists, and we can't say we blame Him.

Another important point to keep in mind is that manliness is inextricably bound up with being an American. Admittedly, there are exceptions to this rule. Attila the Hun, for example, was a man *par excellence,* even though he was not, strictly speaking, an American. But then, he was comporting himself across Europe before there was such a thing as the United States, so it's possible to make an exception in his case. Once the Declaration of Independence was signed, however, a homeland for manliness on earth was finally established. After all, it's no coincidence that Clint Eastwood is not a Russian.

The fact is that America is, always has been, and always will be a man's country. Just take a quick look at American history. Who did all the hard work in settling this great nation of ours? Who took the land away from the Indians? Who kicked the Mexicans out of Texas? Who got rid of all those

nonfunctional trees and other roadblocks to progress and built the greatest system of interstate highways the human race has ever known? Men! And not just men but *real men*—like Davy Crockett, Jim Bowie, Teddy Roosevelt, and Duke Wayne. Sure, women have made important contributions to American culture. If it hadn't been for a woman, who would have sewn the American flag? The fact is, though, that, when you get right down to it, America is a country of men, by men, and for men—and if any of you ladies out there don't like it, why don't you just pack up your Gucci luggage and move to France where you belong?

Now that we've established man's place in God's universal scheme, it's time to turn our attention to more down-to-earth matters: namely, the specific procedures for comportment in everyday life. Comportment is a complex art that takes some men years to master, but with the aid of our easy-to-follow instructions, the reader should begin to notice definite changes in his behavior, personality, and intelligence quotient in no time at all.

If there is one, central maxim to guide today's man down the winding trail of practical comportment, it is this: A man's gotta do what a man's gotta do. Once fully comprehended, this law can be applied to every phase of manly life and serve as a moral compass to keep the reader on the straight and narrow path in work and in play, in body and in mind.

A perfect illustration of this maxim can be found in that supremely manful movie, *The Dirty Dozen*. At the conclusion of this film, Lee Marvin doesn't

really want to send his commando squad on a suicide mission behind enemy lines, but a man's gotta do what a man's gotta do, and he does it. And he's glad he does it. And so are the commandos, who end up getting shot to pieces. Because they're men, too. The crucial lesson to be learned from this example is that, in order to make sure that you are being a man, you should find something that you don't want to do and then do it.

As stirring as this example may be, the reader should not let it gull him into thinking that a man can only comport himself under the extreme test of war (although, to be honest, a good war never hurt anybody). Every civilian male, caught up in the humdrum routine of peacetime existence, must adhere to no less demanding a standard of behavior. For the true man, the trick is to transform his work, his play, and, most important of all, his domestic life, into a daily battlefield, to make everything he does, no matter how seemingly trivial, a test of his manly essence. Never forget, comportment begins in the home: in the way you read the paper in the morning, the way you deal with a leaky faucet, the way you ask the wife for a cup of coffee. You could be the most combat-hardened Joe in the world, but if you can't cut the mustard in the kitchenette, you're strictly Absent Without Leave from manhood.

But how, you may ask, can I remain firm and rigid in my comportment, never letting it slacken for a moment, even in the privacy of my own home? The key to manly comportment is simply to ask yourself at every moment of the day whether what you are doing, or are thinking about doing, is manly. When, in the morning, you are about to sit down to breakfast, you should ask yourself: Is what I am about to eat manly? (If you are about to eat anything other than a steak, fried eggs, a mess of home fried potatoes, a pile of flapjacks, and black coffee, the answer is no.) When you step up to the mirror to shave, you should ask yourself: Am I about to shave in approved manly fashion? (If you shave with anything other than a straight razor, lukewarm water, and little bits of toilet paper to stick onto your face where you nick yourself, the answer is also no.) When you lie down in bed at night, the last thought that should cross your mind before you fall asleep is:

Am I about to sleep in a manly way? (If you can feel the contours of your .357 Magnum pressing against your cheek through the foam rubber of your pillow, the answer is yes.)

When you put down this book, the comportment test for the rest of your life will begin. You are going to have to know how to walk, talk, sit, stand, and think like a man. To that end, we are providing here an illustrated guide to all the fundamentals of manly behavior. Study them carefully. We'll be checking up later on.

Max:
There's only one thing important to me.

Priest:
Finding and killing a man. Primitive, hopeless revenge.

Max:
I'll settle for that.

Priest:
Why, when there's another half of you waiting to be discovered? You also inherited the refined traditions of religion, philosophy, and conscience.

Max:
I don't understand them words.

Steve McQueen as Max Sand in the movie *Nevada Smith*

BASIC TRAINING: HOW TO WALK, TALK, SIT, STAND, AND, IN GENERAL, ACT LIKE A MAN

You don't need a Ph.D. to know that men act differently from women. (In fact, if you have a Ph.D., you're probably some kind of gutless wonder who doesn't even *know* the difference between men and women.) Even children are aware that there are crucial distinctions between the sexes. Young boys, for example, have a simple but effective masculinity test that they will administer to any new male kid on the block to see if he's got what it takes to become a member of their little group and join them in such manly boy's activities as team sports, swapping baseball cards, and jumping the smaller kids in school for their lunch money.

The boy under review is asked to perform a few simple acts: examine his fingernails, cross his legs, look up at the sky. If he performs them correctly, he's okay. If he messes up on even one of them, he's the kind of pansy who should trade in his Converse All-Stars for a pair of Mary Janes and seriously consider signing up for the Campfire Girls. (For those non-manly readers who don't instinctively know the correct way of doing these things, here are the answers:

Men look at their nails by turning their hands palm upward and curling over their fingers; women do it by looking at the back of their hands with the fingers stuck straight out. Men cross their legs by resting the ankle of the top leg on the knee of the bottom one; women do it by crossing their thighs. Men look at the sky by glancing upward with as little head movement as possible; women do it by tilting their heads all the way back.)

Now there is a profound truth embodied in this unassuming test: namely, that men must follow certain inflexible rules of behavior in the performance of every task, from those that are fairly easy to master, such as checking out your fingernails, to ones that are relatively more complex, such as launching a ground war in Asia. Obviously, we will not be able to cover every contingency in this book; to determine how a real man would act in any given situation, you'll either have to rely on the handy "manly self-examination" method we outlined earlier or watch a lot of old Robert Mitchum movies. Still, there are certain fundamental activities that are so critical, because they are encountered so often in the course of one's life (walking, for example), that we would be derelict in our duty if we did not offer the following, exhaustively detailed description of how they are performed by real men.

MANLY EXTRA
LESSON NUMBER ONE: HOW TO
STAND LIKE A MAN

1 How to Walk Like a Man

Place one foot firmly and unflinchingly in front of the other while keeping your stomach sucked in, your chest thrust out, and your shoulders held rigidly back. Just as important as the proper physical execution of perambulation is maintaining the correct mental and spiritual perspective during the act. Let's say that you're walking down the street and you see some guy coming towards you from the opposite direction. Just keep on marching along in your usual gutsy, unswerving style, and if he doesn't want to get knocked down and tromped on, let *him* move out of the way. In short, the basic rule of manly walking is: A man never steps aside (although there are several things you might want to consider making exceptions for, among them white-haired old ladies with arthritis, children in strollers, and brick walls).

2 How to Talk Like a Man

First, you talk like a man by speaking only when you have to, and even then only in the most cryptic manner possible. As a rule, a man does not volunteer information. It's just not natural. Of course, when he is in a bar with half a bag on, it's perfectly okay for him to go on at exhaustive length about how he broke his collarbone in his last year of high school basketball. This is one of several circumstances in which talking is not only appropriate but highly commendable in a man. More about the other verbal situations that may arise in a man's life in later chapters.

The standards of manhood

MANLY EXTRA
THE MANLY WAY OF
ENTERING A HOUSE

MANLY BONUS

HOW TO TALK LIKE A MAN

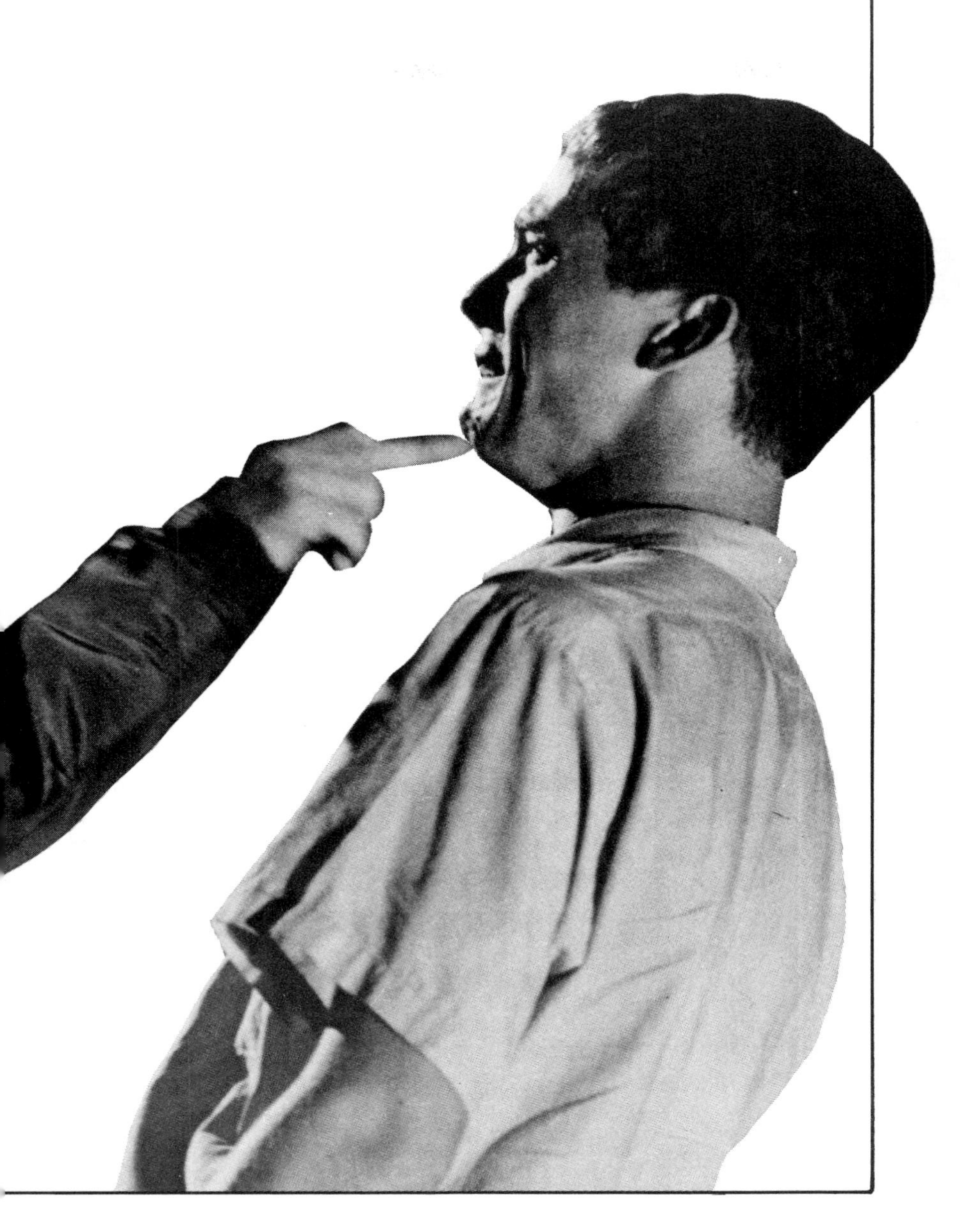

require that you know not only when to talk but what physical gestures should accompany your words. Ideally, a man should punctuate his sentences by jabbing the listener's chest with a stiff index finger while spitting cigarette smoke in the guy's face.

3 How to Sit Like a Man

Place your feet squarely on the floor and keep a firm hold on the armrests. If no armrests immediately present themselves, you may fold your arms across your chest Indian-fashion. Preferably, the sitting man should position himself with either his back against the wall or his front facing a mirror. Wild Bill Hickok sat with his back to the room one time and never committed that particular oversight again, mainly because someone walked up behind him and shot him in the head. While this presented Wild Bill with the kind of opportunity every man lives for—the chance to show that he could take it like a man—it was still an aggravating way of learning a relatively simple lesson. Can you afford to make the same mistake?

It's permissible to sit with your legs crossed, provided that you use the approved manly position (see above). Under no circumstances, however, should you sit with your hands folded in your lap. When you are in a crowded, public place—a movie theater, for example, or a bus—the preferred way to sit is with your feet placed firmly on the floor and your knees spread as far apart as possible. In this way, you will not only establish your dominance over the territory you are occupying, but if there is a doll sitting on either side of you, you will also be able to indulge in a little suave manly flirtation by rubbing one of your legs against one of hers. *(Caution!* If there is a *man* sitting on either side of you, you will be forced to modify this position somewhat or run the risk of having one of your legs touch that of another male, in

MANLY EXTRA

HOW TO SMILE LIKE A MAN

MANLY EXTRA

THE MANLY WAY TO SECURE A BANK LOAN

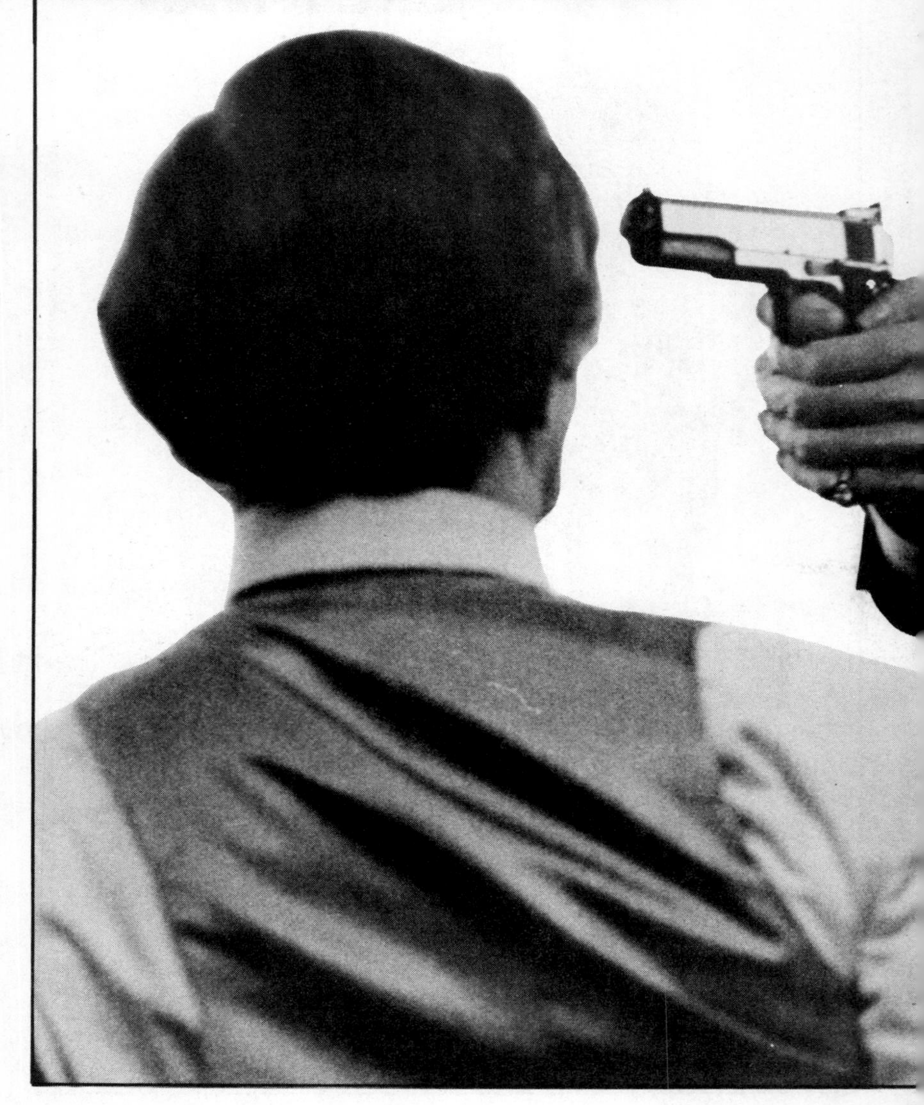

which case you are probably some kind of homo and should seriously consider going straight home and taking your own life.)

Once you have mastered these basics, feel free to improvise. A rigid, militaristic posture or a glowering slouch may be just the thing for you. Express yourself. But express yourself manfully.

4 How to Sleep Like a Man

A man may sleep in one of two ways: (1) flat on his back, absolutely rigid, one eye open, right hand gripping the .357 Magnum hidden beneath the pillow; or (2) spread all over the mattress in a drunken sprawl. In order to insure the full visual impact of the latter alternative, tangled sheets are imperative. Refrain from making your bed for several months until the desired rumpled look is attained. Regardless of which option you choose, a full, resonant snore should be cultivated.

MANLY EXTRA
HOW TO
SMOKE
LIKE A MAN

WHAT THE WELL-DRESSED MAN IS WEARING

We live in a world that places a high premium on appearances. Given the frenetic pace of modern life and the number of hours you have to put in to earn enough money for the really important things—T-bone steaks, beer, and X-rated video cassettes—there just isn't enough time to get to know other people. Judging others by the clothes they wear has become the easiest and most logical way of getting around this problem. In order, therefore, to let people know exactly where you're coming from, you must dress the part of a man. No matter how much of a man you may be in your soul, if you don't have the threads to prove it, then you're just plain out of uniform, trooper.

As we will soon demonstrate, there is a wide variety of comportmental clothing available to men, but for the fledgling aspirant to manhood we will begin by outlining those simple items of apparel that should form the basis of any truly virile wardrobe. The essentials of manly attire include work boots; a plaid flannel shirt; a pair of grubby, undesigned jeans; a mackinaw jacket; and a .38 Smith & Wesson. For a night out on the town, the fundamentals would consist of work boots; a plaid flannel shirt; a pair of grubby, undesigned jeans; a blue blazer with a U.S. Olympics emblem sewn onto the breast pocket; and a .38 Smith & Wesson. The reader should make sure he has purchased all of these basic articles of clothing before he begins spending money on more elaborate togs, such as camouflage jackets and hip waders.

Just as important to the beginner as knowing what to wear is knowing exactly what to avoid at all cost. Since fashions and the tides of social change are constantly shifting (and way too often, as far as we're concerned), the suitability of certain styles of dress is sometimes

STYLE NOTE

For a carefree day on the town with your pals, a jaunty, devil-may-care look is just the thing. A pair of matching leather, studded wrist bands will put you in the center of any picture.

CASUAL LOOK

This year more than ever, the casual look is going to be big, Big, BIG. Whether you're in or out of stir, workshirts, denim pants, and a loaded rod will be your passport to any occasion.

One look at this duo and you know they are ready to comport. The man on the left clearly recognizes the importance of a sweat-soaked hatband and mud-encrusted boots, while his buddy on the right understands the intrinsic value of a necktie worn backwards and a suit that has been carefully slept in for a week.

MIX AND MATCH

TIES ARE IN

For the man who knows the meaning of pure, animal magnetism, a pruned head and a string tie can speak volumes.

HATS MAKE THE MAN

No man is complete without a snappy chapeau in his wardrobe. Hats such as these just plain look good on anybody.

THE MILITARY CUT

Nothin' fancy, thanks, and proud of it. When you just want to get out into the field, what could be finer than the casual look from Uncle Sam?

LEISURE STYLE

When it's time to get back in civvies, make a big bang with the look that says, "Go ahead and try me, sport. See what it'll get ya." Sure to catch the eye of any dame worth a tumble.

EARS ARE IN

Clothes may make the man, but even the classiest duds won't do you any good without an attractive haircut to go with them.

FATHER-AND-SON LOOK

The father-and-son look is back. Give your boy a sense of manly companionship and a style that money can't buy.

MANLY FASHIONS ON PARADE

ON THE TOWN

An important business engagement to attend? Make sure you make the right impression with togs from True Sicilian of Chicago?

ACCESSORIES MAKE THE MAN

For the man who has everything. A timeless outfit that suits any occasion, whether you are out at a fancy-dress dinner party or just lounging around the house. Twenty dollars extra for the female attached to the chest.

DAYTIME CHIC

A monogrammed shirt with rolled-up sleeves is just right for a day on the job . . .

AFTER FIVE

. . . and in the evening, just slip on a snappy, double-breasted jacket and you're all set for a night on the town.

tricky to determine. For instance, leather jackets were once considered extremely manly, but nowadays you shouldn't be caught dead in one. There are just too damn many high flyers and foul balls wearing leather. No sense in taking a chance. The same thing goes for cowboy wear. You won't find anyone who is more of a man than a sure-enough cowboy, but just take a look at any bar where the leather jacket types are hanging out and you'll see more Western boots and ten-gallon hats than you can shake a stick at. If you must dress like a cowboy, our times demand that you do so judiciously. Do not wear fire-engine red boots, do not wear Western shirts embroidered with chartreuse flowers, and refrain from strapping on a bra.

Other important don't's for the manly dresser: Don't wear a sweater tied around your neck, avoid ascots as much as possible, do not wear dungarees without a belt (the belt should be no less than three inches wide), and pass up any opportunity to slip into brightly colored bikini briefs. And finally, if you're going to wear a tie, don't walk around the streets with an open collar and a loose knot. If you can't take wearing a tight collar, you might as well throw away the tie and get yourself a dress.

In regard to the full range of fashions available to men: there is a vast array of snappy styles and spiffy combinations for the individual with enough money to spend. We don't propose to describe them all here, since we would only be repeating the information that can be found in that bible on matters of manly attire, *The Manly Warehouse Catalog*. This indispensable sourcebook covers in matchless detail everything that should be included in this year's manly wardrobe. In deference to this acknowledged authority, and with the permission of its compilers, we are reprinting the illustrated highlights from this year's volume.

The first part of the day is just like a game day. I get the paper, drink my coffee. I really notice it around three o'clock, when I should be heading to the park. Everybody says, "How do you like your vacation?" To me, a vacation is playing ball and being with the guys.

Rick Cerone, catcher for the New York Yankees, during the 1981 baseball strike

MANLY ACCESSORIES

Among the various fashion accessories that will give an added dash of manliness to your appearance, the three most highly recommended are facial scars, eye patches, and tattoos.

Heidelberg duelling scars were once considered the height of manliness, but they are difficult to come by in today's world. A perfectly adequate and easy-to-acquire substitute is the kind inflicted by a broken beer bottle during a barroom fight. Eye patches are also highly virile, though they are something of an affectation unless you're actually missing an eye, in which case it's even more manly to walk around with your empty eye socket uncovered.

Tattoos are tricky. An arm tattoo of a heart with the word "Mommy" written inside it, for example, is definitely *not* manly, though for certain mystical reasons the same tattoo with the word "Mother" inscribed inside it *is*. (For more on this matter, see our chapter "Man and His Mother.") A brilliantly colored butterfly tattooed on the inside of your thigh is, needless to say, not manly, though it is a highly desirable adornment for a Man's Woman. (Other favorites are simple inscriptions, tastefully inscribed on the right buttock,

Metallic eye patches are even manlier than the old-fashioned leather kind. The handsome eyepiece pictured here (designed by Augie's of Bakersfield) is particularly arresting when complemented by scruffy sideburns and two layers of grime.

such as "Made in America," "U.S. Prime," and "Property of The Satan's Slaves.")

The most highly recommended manly tattoos are phallic-shaped weapons (spears, daggers, bayonets), any creature that comes equipped with long, drooling fangs or razor-sharp talons (tigers, wolves, cobras, hawks), the initials "U.S.M.C.", bare-breasted hula dancers, and the American flag. The only problem with the latter is that you will be compelled to use the color red in applying it. Manly tattoos shouldn't contain any bright colors, if possible. They should be a uniform sickly blue with the outlines of the image all bleeding together. A truly manly tattoo should look like something you applied to your own forearm, bicep or chest (the only acceptable locations) with a blunt instrument and a bottle of India ink during a really long weekend of drinking.

FRIENDSHIP: THE JOY OF BUDDIES

A man may have friends.

Ideally, of course, a man shouldn't have to depend on anyone. The loner, the rugged, go-it-alone individualist is, perhaps, the truest man of all. Did Alan Ladd ask for volunteers when he set off to wipe out the bad guys in *Shane*? Did Clint Eastwood call for help when he was cleaning up San Francisco in *Dirty Harry*? Not hardly. The fact is, however, that both *Shane* and *Dirty Harry* are works of art, and there is a world of difference between art and real life. In art, you get to gun down assorted slimeballs and long-haired, psycho hippie creeps pretty often. Clint does it about six times per movie. In real life,

however, such an opportunity rarely comes along. Once, maybe. And even then, only if Lady Luck is on your side, especially nowadays when the long-haired, psycho hippie creep has pretty much gone the way of the buffalo.

For this reason, it's perfectly all right for a man to have friends. After all, even Genghis Khan had to call in a horde or two to help get the job done. The stresses and strains of life can be so intense for a man, in fact, that it's not only permissible for him to have friends, it's downright necessary.

You're a pretty good guy—for a girl.

Robert Mitchum in the movie *Angel Face*

Very often, a man is something less than a real man unless he can refer to a bunch of other men as "the boys." One of the first steps to be taken in pursuit of manhood is the cultivation of just such a group, dedicated to the proposition of nonstop comportment. If you don't already have a bunch of guys you can call your own, do not delay in finding one. Call up the old gang from high school, renew friendships from boot camp. If for some reason you don't have any such old contacts to build upon, you'll have to start from scratch: Ask the guys down at work if anyone wants to be your buddy, pop in at the neighborhood pool hall and see what's cooking there, sign up at Jack LaLanne's. You may even be well advised to stop reading right here and only return to this book when this matter has been attended to. It's that important.

When a man wants to go hunting or canoeing down white water or simply wants to drink a lot of beer and talk loud, what is he supposed to do, get a woman? Give us a break. He should get some men. Who else would he be able to share life's manful pleasures with? When you come right down to it, men like to be with men.

When there is a problem on the job or in the home, who are you going to talk to? God knows you can't talk to the wife. You've got to talk to a man, preferably several men. In that way, you will be relieved of any embarrassing need to express your innermost feelings in an intimate manner and can instead forge right ahead to the business of having some hell-bent-for-leather fun. And when

ACCEPTABLE MANLY GREETINGS FOR FRIENDS

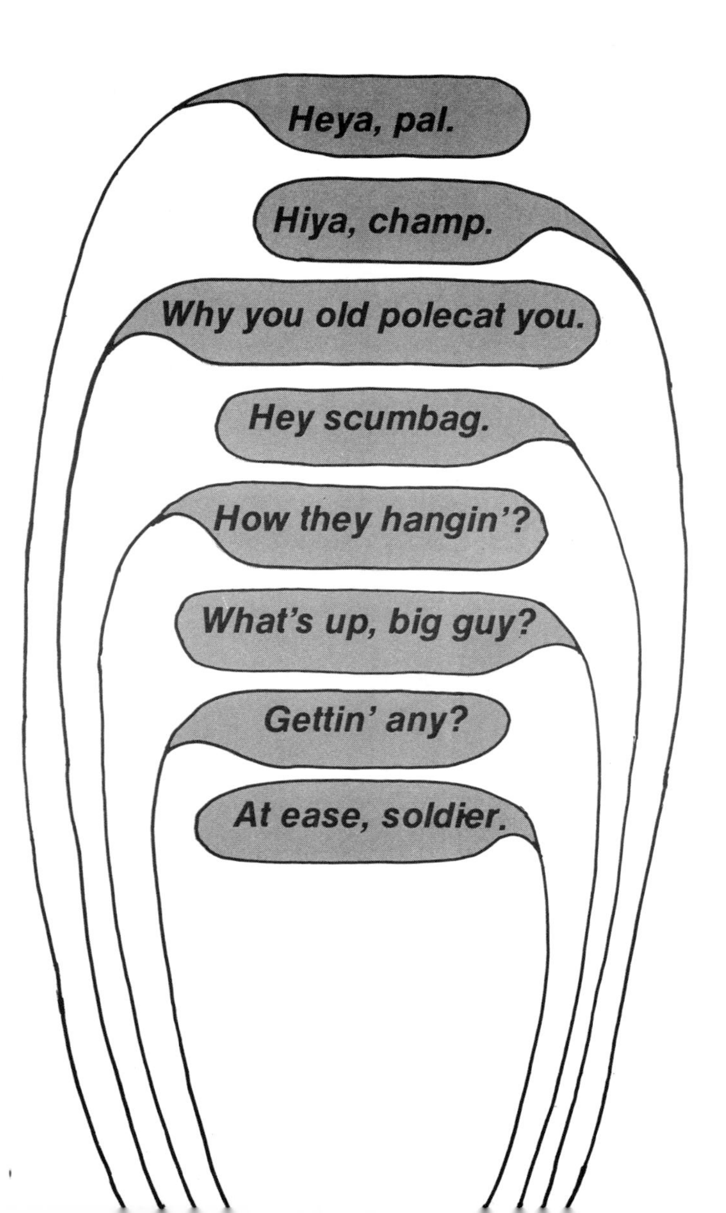

things are going great, who better to celebrate with than the boys? No matter what the circumstances, you can't go too far wrong with your buddies. And the activities don't have to be very elaborate either. Mountain climbing and sky-diving are infinitely commendable, but you can do just as well sitting around on a Sunday afternoon with the guys, hoisting a few and watching the game. In your own little way, you'll be standing up for America.

THE MAN'S WOMAN

Without any doubt, there is a place for a woman in this man's world. But she has to be a certain kind of woman—a man's woman. Of the other kind (a woman's woman) there are plenty, in fact, too damn many. You see women bucking for a promotion in the company, working their way through medical school, running for public office, opening car doors for themselves. Where's it going to end? Next thing you know, they'll be sitting on the Supreme Court.

It's a simple fact for all to see that a woman can never be a man no matter what Betty Friedan may try to tell you. Only a man can be a man. On the other hand, if she plays her cards right, a female just may be man enough to be a real woman, which is exactly what any self-respecting man is looking for. This latter variety of female is known in manly terminology as a man's woman.

A man's woman appreciates a real man and is just as likely to gag at the sight of a male buying a ticket to the Joffrey Ballet as any man would be. She won't break off a date to attend an emergency meeting of her consciousness-raising group (mainly because she doesn't belong to a conscious-

MANLY BONUS
A BEVY OF MEN'S WOMEN

RIGS
FOR
HIRE
7222-14

ness-raising group), would much rather go see *Magnum Force* than *Kramer vs. Kramer,* and has never heard of Sylvia Plath. A man's woman knows how to do those little things that make a man happy, like keeping the latest issue of *Mechanix Illustrated* in her bathroom at all times. And when Saturday night rolls around, she is just as pleased as she can be to stay home with her man and watch pro wrestling on the tube. She'll do all these things and more because, well, because that's just the kind of guy she is.

Those who have already read the preceding chapter on friendship may very well find a vexing question taking shape in their minds at this point. If, as we have stated, a man mostly likes to be with other men, then what would he see in a woman, no matter what kind she is?

True enough, a man likes to be with men, but in a man's woman, he sees some glimmer of manly qualities, however watered-down they may be. When you call up your girl and say, "I'll be three hours late for our date, babe, because I feel like bendin' elbows with the guys down at the bar, and that's that," and she says, "That's okay. I'll wait for you," that's the man in her talking.

When she's got some womanly problem—she's pregnant, she got fired from her job because the boss found a secretary who can type faster, her aged mother just passed away—a man's woman doesn't go running to her man and laying it all on him. A man can't be bothered with that. He's got his own problems. Maybe the Yankee game just got rained out, or the carburetor on his Chevy is acting up again. If she's man enough to be a woman, she should be man enough to tough things out on her own.

A man's woman is many things to many men but there's one thing she definitely is *not,* and that's Jill Clayburgh. The woman's woman who proliferates in our age and flaunts her rights as if she had a legitimate claim to them is indeed a distressing spectacle to any fine, upstanding American who values decency, free enterprise, and strategic air superiority over Libya. But the situation is not hopeless. A man's woman may be hard to find in today's out-of-whack world, but the trouble you take to acquire one will be well worth your while. Just keep your eyes peeled for that special gal who is man enough to be the woman every man craves. You won't be sorry.

MAN AND HIS MOTHER

The last label you could affix to a man is "mamma's boy." On the other hand, a man is never anything less than a model son. A man respects the lasting values that have made this country great, and surely there is nothing more valuable than Motherhood, except possibly for private enterprise, the right to bear arms, and dispensing free birth control pills to teenage girls. When a mother gives birth to a man, she is gaining an untiring protector and provider, someone she can always rely on, someone who will fly to her aid at a moment's notice, even if it's his bowling night. (During league championships

> ***I still held his automatic more or less pointed at him, but he swung on me just the same. It caught me flush on the chin. I back-stepped fast enough to keep from falling, but I took plenty of the punch. It was meant to be a hard one, but a pansy has no iron in his bones whatever he looks like.***
>
> **Philip Marlowe in Raymond Chandler's *The Big Sleep***

you must use your own judgement.)

A man's first obligation to his mother is to defend her honor when he is in the company of other men. Customarily, this takes the form of beating to a pulp anyone who should refer to her in even a slightly irreverent tone. But this is only a start. It is not enough simply to make sure that your sainted mother's name isn't taken in vain; the mere mention of the phrase "your mother" by another man is sufficient cause for a bonecrushing headlock and a swift right jab to the solar plexis. The remark "Your mother wears combat boots" is, of course, an occasion for justifiable homicide.

Your next obligation is to remember your mother on her birthday. There are many manly things you can do to make this day something special for her, a day she will cherish in her memory forever. A gift will usually do the trick. Many choices are open to you: you might want to give her an ashtray fashioned out of a hub cap, a season's pass to the Boston Bruins home games, or perhaps a new tire jack, so that she can learn to change flats by herself. You might even do something extra special like having "Mom" tattooed on your bicep. Almost any gift will do, as long as the right feeling is there. And remember, it's not only the expensive presents that will clinch the day for Mom. Certain things just can't be measured in material terms. As a matter of fact, it might not even be necessary to buy her a gift at all; there are so many other ways of saying, "I love you." On some birthdays, the best thing you can do for the old lady is simply to come over to her place and let her cook dinner for you. To show her that you really care, you can bring along a bottle of Irish

You went out there to talk. Why did you kill him?

Guess the conversation just kinda dried up, ma'am.

John Wayne in the movie *The Undefeated*, after shooting a Mexican bandito he didn't much like the looks of.

Manly Gifts for Your Children

Catcher's Mitt
Soldering Iron
Subscription to Hustler
Skates (Hockey Style)
Junior-size Crossbow
Power Drill
Day Trip to West Point
Membership in Your Gun Club
Year's Supply of Trojans

whiskey, so that the next time you visit she won't have to run out and buy something for you to drink.

The last obligation you have to your mother is never to call her. In this way, she won't have to lie awake at night, wondering if she did a good job of raising you. By never calling, you'll be showing her that you can stand on your own two feet. It's your way of saying, "Thanks, Mom, for a job well done!" A man just thinks of these things.

MANLY EXTRA

MY LIFE WITH A "REAL" MAN

MANLY RETORTS

Again and again in our distressingly feminized times, real men find themselves barraged by snide remarks, insults, and impertinent questions from women of both sexes. Obviously a man can't suffer such disrespect in silence, but what can he do when the letter of the law seems to frown on putting punks like these in a full body cast? The answer in the majority of cases is the skillful use of manly retorts—simple and direct verbal stingers designed to end any unwanted discussions pronto. Grown men (or rather grown-up adults of the male gender pretending to be men) have been known to fold up and mince away in tears in the face of such snappy comebacks.

An example: let's say some "sensitive" young fellow comes up to you and sneers, "Hey, like, are you on some kind of macho trip, man?" You just look him in the eye and say, "Back off, Clarence. Your slip is showing." You can be sure that he'll keep his distance from there on in. Or maybe a woman approaches you and says, "You think you're a real tough guy, don't you? You think you can walk all over everybody." Just turn right around with, "Yeah, well at least I'm not a dyke." End of discussion. She's gotten the message. Score one for America.

Naturally, we don't expect you to be able to come up with such masterful *bon mots* all by yourself on the spur of the moment, so we have provided some all-purpose manly retorts that will serve in a wide variety of situations.

Below is a sampling of some uncalled-for remarks and the appropriate manly responses to them.

"Hey, what're you doing parking in my garden?"

"What's it to you?"

"It's three o'clock in the morning. Where were you all night?"

"What's it to you?"

"Excuse me, but that's my foot you're stepping on."

"What's it to you?"

Another equally versatile weapon in a man's repertoire of comebacks is "Says you," a retort that is capable of shooting down a whole host of impertinent comments.

"Nixon never should have been pardoned."

"Says you."

"Football is boring."

"Says you."

"You can't just drive all over my front lawn and expect to get away with it!"

"Says you."

If someone insults you in print, a verbal retort may not be sufficient. It may be necessary to fall back on the time-honored tradition of making him eat his words.

If either of these barbs should fail to do the job and the opposition comes back at you with some measly wisecrack, you can lay the issue to rest with a devastating, "You and what army?"

For those of you who don't care to bother with sorting out which particular retort goes with which category of provocation, there are two time-tested lines that are bound to cover any given situation. Anytime you feel that some undesirable is violating your personal manly space with some fool question, just look him in the eye and say, "Oh yeah?" or, if that doesn't do the trick, "Who wants to know?" With these two unbeatable toppers at your fingertips, just let someone try to get the better of *you*. He'll be sorry he did.

THE MANLY ADVISOR

Dear Manly Advisor:
I'm in my freshman year at college and I share a dorm room with this guy on the football team. When I see my roommate getting dressed, I get this strange feeling. I'm beginning to think I'm attracted to him. Is there something wrong with me?—B.P., Kansas City, MO.

Is there something wrong with you? Nothing that locking yourself in your room with a .44 automatic and blowing your goddamn brains out won't cure, you slimeball.

Dear Manly Advisor:
I notice that when I go out and beat up homosexuals at night, I get sexually excited. Is there something wrong with me?
—J.L., Boston, MA.

No.

Dear Manly Advisor:
I recently purchased a mini-component system with signal-strength indicator, defeatable FM interstation muting, Super ANRS feature to extend dynamic range in treble, and quartz tuner with manual frequency scan. I notice when I use it, however, that there is a certain amount of intermodular distortion. What do you advise?
—P.R., West Lafayette, IN

Hey, what am I supposed to be, Mr. Wizard or something? Figure it out for yourself, Einstein.

Dear Manly Advisor:
I am a healthy twenty-four-year-old woman with boyfriend problems. I am writing because I know there are some things that only a man can answer. Sexually I am very inventive and my boyfriend is very straight. Sexually I like to try all sorts of things that I read about in *New Woman* magazine and I would like my boyfriend to include one of his buddies in our lovemaking, but my boyfriend isn't into it. How can I persuade him? After all, what's wrong with trying new things?
—D.N. New York, N.Y.

You make me sick.

GREAT MOMENTS IN MANHOOD

G. Gordon Liddy builds up his willpower by cooking the second joint of his left index finger over a burning candle.

✱✱✱✱✱✱✱✱✱✱✱

Lord Raglan orders the charge of the Light Brigade. Anyone can win a battle when he has a clear strategic advantage, but it takes a real man to send his troops riding headfirst into a line of blazing artillery just for the heck of it.

✱✱✱✱✱✱✱✱✱✱✱

G. Gordon Liddy continues to build up his willpower by burning a 1½-by-2-inch hole in his forearm with a match. Go for it, Gordo!

✱✱✱✱✱✱✱✱✱✱✱

Western outlaw John Wesley Hardin shoots a man in an adjacent hotel room in Abilene because the guy was snoring. A man can put up with only so much.

✱✱✱✱✱✱✱✱✱✱✱

Smacky Jack, legendary president of the Satan's Slaves motorcycle gang, knocks down a waitress who has refused to serve him coffee and extracts three of her teeth with a rusty pair of pliers that he carries around expressly for this purpose. Later, finding himself parched but penniless in a bar, he pulls out one of his own teeth and offers to trade it for a drink. That Smacky Jack—what a crazy guy.

✱✱✱✱✱✱✱✱✱✱✱

Late, great Dodger centerfielder Pete Reiser runs into the outfield wall for the final time. Considered in the 1940s to be one of the most gifted players in the National League, Reiser had to retire prematurely due to his habit of crashing into the centerfield wall when chasing fly balls. You gotta hand it to Reiser. He was a real man. He knew what he wanted and went after it and didn't let obstacles stand in his way.

✱✱✱✱✱✱✱✱✱✱✱

Genghis Khan's life.

✱✱✱✱✱✱✱✱✱✱✱

Star pitcher Juan Marichal of the San Francisco Giants clubs

Dodger catcher John Roseboro with a baseball bat for no apparent reason in the middle of the 1965 season.

★★★★★★★★★★

Wyatt Earp leads the fight against the Clanton-McLowery gang at the O.K. Corral. Certain sissified historians like to harp on the fact that two of the three members of the Clanton-McLowery gang shot down that day were completely unarmed. All right, so Wyatt made a couple of mistakes. Big deal. As any real man will tell you, a few misfits accidentally knocked off now and then is a small price to pay for law and order.

G. Gordon Liddy volunteers to kill his friend and co-conspirator E. Howard Hunt after Hunt decides to give evidence to the other side. A man doesn't wait to be asked to be a man.

★★★★★★★★★★

General George Patton slaps two soldiers in a field hospital who are complaining of combat fatigue. Some bleeding-heart critics, obviously acting on orders from Moscow, accused Patton of unwarranted brutality. Hell, anyone could see those boys were just bellyaching, and old "Blood and Guts" was man enough to call their bluff.

PHOTO QUIZ #1

FIND THE REAL MEN

Interspersed throughout this book are a number of quizzes designed to test your progress as you travel the long road towards true manliness. If you've been paying close attention and following instructions, you should be able to handle this one pretty easily. (We might note, however, that, as a rule, following instructions isn't manly. Real men are leaders, not followers. They go their own way. However, since you're never going to be a man unless you listen to everything we say, you'll have to hold that particular rule in abeyance for a while. Once you've absorbed all our lessons and are prepared to go it alone, you can pass this book along to some needy friend, though it would be more manly to buy him his own copy.)

Instructions: Study the following photographs carefully, then try to identify the man.

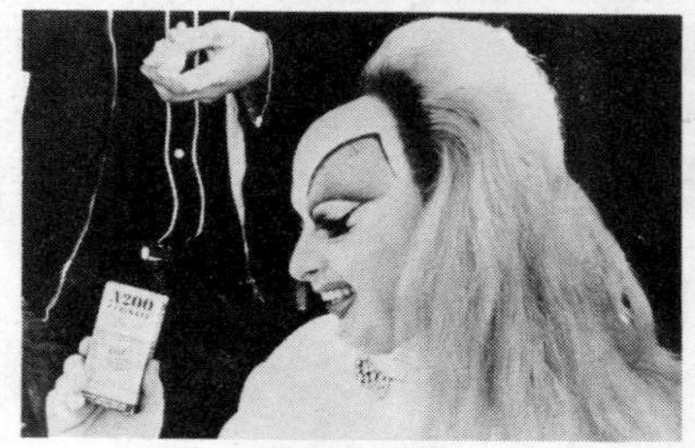

The answer to this quiz will be found on page 44 of the sequel to this book.

PART TWO

MAN ALONE

SEX AND THE SINGLE MAN

In order to keep fit both in body and mind, it is imperative that the young single man have sex on a regular basis. Whether he does it with a casual pick-up or someone he actually knows, the reader should keep all his juices moving and exercise every vital part. As essential as this practice is, however, the reader will undoubtedly notice that certain parts of this chapter are something less than explicit, particularly when it comes to the mechanics of the sex act itself. The reason for this is very simple. In the matter of raw, unbridled sex, no real man should have to consult a book, not even this book. It is a well-known fact that how-to sex manuals are strictly for women and children. Even if an aspiring man feels he has something to learn in this regard, he should go about it in the proper comportmental fashion. Remember, there's nothing that can be learned from a book that can't be learned better from hanging around a pool hall or sitting through a couple of showings of *Debbie Does Dallas.*

Our main concern in this section, therefore, will be to explain the elaborate rituals that surround sexual relations and how a man should negotiate these obstacles. A flourishing

MANLY EXTRA

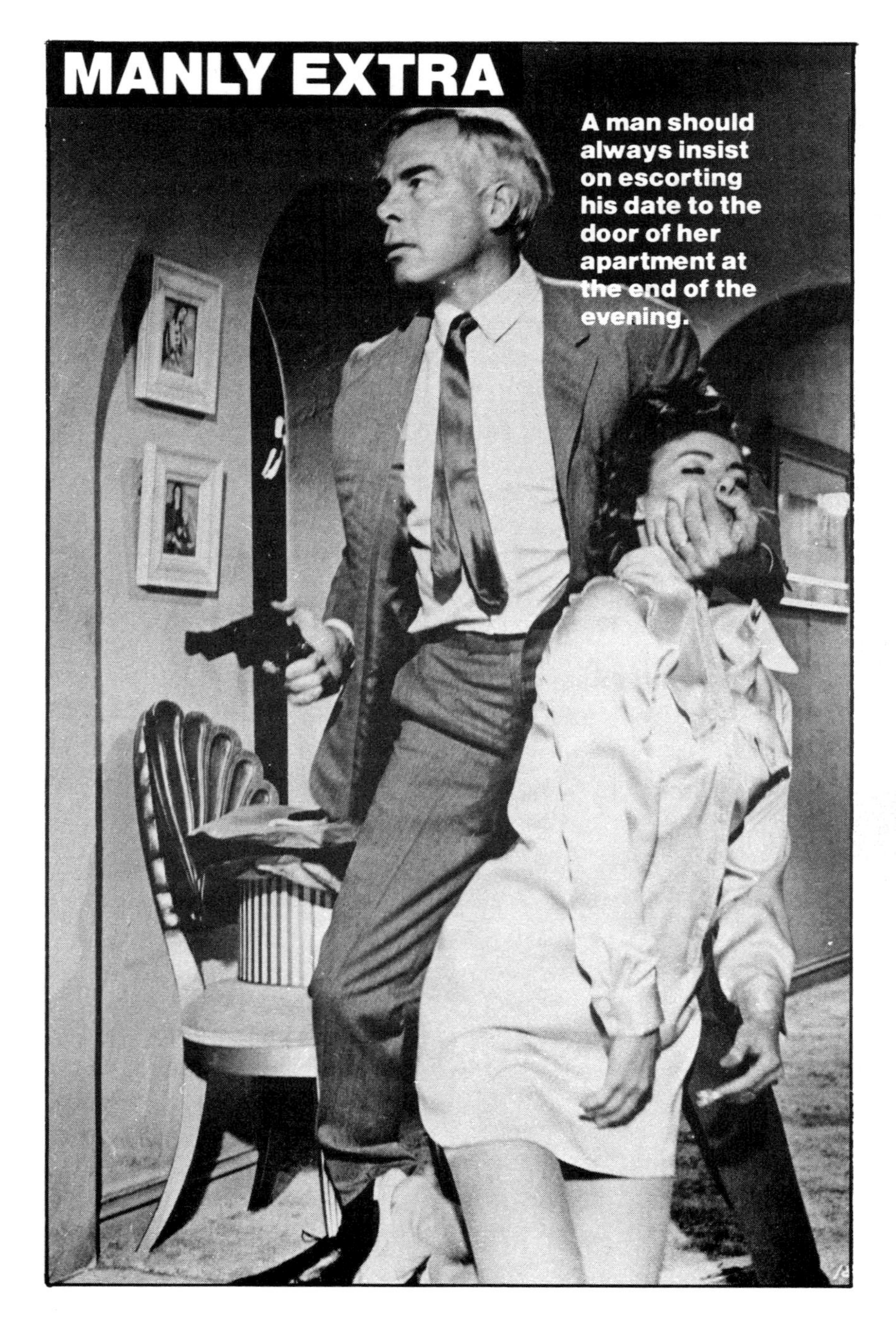

A man should always insist on escorting his date to the door of her apartment at the end of the evening.

singles scene exists in our society; much of this scene does not conform to strict manly standards, but it is with us nonetheless. If you're going on a fishing trip in those waters, you'll need more than a hook, some bait, and a sturdy pole. Our job is to provide you with a navigational chart that will make the trip smooth sailing and allow you to drop your anchor in the port of your choice.

Say you're a young, unattached male with a flair for the virile and a demonstrated readiness to go nose-to-nose with the Russkies at a moment's notice. You are looking for some casual sexual exercise, so you set out at approximately twenty-two-hundred hours for the local singles bar. Obviously you're going to be an object of unbounded passion for any female with her sense organs intact, but how do you go about presenting yourself so that your sexual charisma comes across most clearly in a jaded singles hangout? Comportment in such a setting requires expert judgement and an infallible sense of timing.

The single most important technique to use in such a situation is the fine art of what is known as Giving-the-Brush.

If you're at a fancy East Side singles bar, don't let yourself be pressured into making a hasty choice. Take your time to check out the field.

Contrary to popular opinion, a man doesn't score in a singles bar by moving in on a skirt and handing her a lot of pick-up lines. He doesn't want to come across like some kind of he-flirt. His first order of business is simply to go to the bar and get himself a drink, either beer or bourbon on the rocks. Let the namby-pambies think what they will, but a bar is there for drinking, first and foremost, as far as a man is concerned.

Just pick up your glass, position yourself in a strategic spot, and let the chips fall where they may. You're in no hurry. You know that you've got what it takes, so you're just going to stand your ground and let the dolls know that a man is amongst them. This initial waiting period may range from a few minutes to several hours, depending on the layout of the place, the demographics of the crowd, the position of the moon, and how many girls pass you on the way to the can. To while away some of this time, you might want to find a guy drinking Perrier and discreetly kick him in the shins.

Sooner or later some doll is going to waltz on over and make a play for you; you can bet even-money on it. And when she does, that's when you roll into action. Right away you've got to give her the brush. When she starts speaking to you, you can't just stand there and let her lead you into a conversation. You don't want to come off like a sap. You give her the brush. You've got to show her what kind of stuff you're made of right from the get-go. A wimp doesn't know enough to act bored when some luscious babe throws herself at him, but a man is smarter than that. He's man enough to turn on the deep freeze and show her that he's the one who's calling the shots. He brushes her off.

Exactly how you brush her off is not important, as long as she is good and brushed. When she comes over and begins talking about how crowded the bar is, for example, you might say, "Beat it, I'm busy," or "Walk east till your hat floats, babe." Whatever you say, if she's a real Man's Woman, she'll respect you for it. It's all very simple, really: when you give her the brush, she knows she's talking to a real man, and when you see that she's man enough to take a brush, you know she's your kind of woman.

If you doubt the validity of any of this, just refer to any Mike Hammer detective novel by Mickey Spillane. Where would Mike be if he folded up every time some curvy dame threw a pass at him? In Chumpsville, that's where. As a remarkably astute character in Paddy Chayevsky's *Marty* so aptly observed, "What I like about Mickey Spillane is he knows how to handle women." Spoken like a man, about a man.

Once you've allowed a half-dozen or so girls to receive the brush, you proceed to make your move. First, choose the woman you're going to take home. This decision should be based on one of two criteria: (1) which girl is the best looking; or (2) which one is throwing you the most blatant pass. As for the first criterion, we leave the final judgement up to you. Beauty is in the eye of the beholder and all that, though offhand we'd say that if the candidate bears even a passing resemblance to Debbie Harry, go ahead and give it a shot. If you're basing your choice on the second option, however, a few manly tips may be in order.

How can you tell if a woman is throwing you a pass? Imagine for a moment that you are standing in our hypothetical singles bar, checking out the scene. Here comes a skirt who's obviously polished off one too many Pink Ladies. Giggling at every misstep, she weaves drunkenly across the floor and blindly staggers into you. This is a pass. It was no accident that she ran into you, all her cheap theatrics to the contrary. It's her way of saying, "I'm out of control; do with me what you will." Even so, as hungry for you as she so clearly is, there's no reason to let yourself be railroaded into anything. Take your time to consider the rest of the field. Over by the bar, some chippie is tapping her foot restlessly and periodically checking her watch. She seems tired of this place, anxious to get going. This, too, is a pass. Any time you see a woman in a bar looking at her watch, you can be sure she's throwing you a pass. It's crucial to be able to pick up on signals like this, to be able to read the subtle meanings concealed in these seemingly insignificant gestures. What she is saying by looking at her watch is "I can't stand it any longer. When are you going to come home with me?" This ploy constitutes a greater pass than the aforementioned drunken stagger. Still, you don't want to be rash and leap to a decision. Take a swallow of brew, lean back against the bar,

PLAYING IT COOL

Giving women the brush is a tradition that goes back to the very beginning of our country. When he wasn't too busy bringing law and order to the old West by pistol-whipping any miscreant who looked at him cross-eyed, Wyatt Earp liked nothing better than to sit back, relax, and give some dancehall babe the brush.

and glance around. Another girl walks over to where you are standing and starts chatting flirtatiously with the guy right next to you. She's trying to make you jealous. A definite pass. A play for jealousy is even more blatant than an expression of impatience. As anxious as you might be by now to make your move, however, you should take just one final look around to be absolutely sure. Now you notice that standing in the far corner next to the cigarette machine is a skirt who refuses to so much as glance in your direction. The old playing-hard-to-get routine. This babe wants you so bad that she won't even look at you for fear that she'll go all to pieces. You are now witnessing the supreme pass. This doll is the one for you.

Picking up a woman under these circumstances is mere

MANLY BONUS

THE HIGHLY EROTIC "SPINNING-AROUND" MOVE AS DEMONSTRATED BY THE MASTER

child's play; it shouldn't be necessary for us to outline the procedure for you. If you can't figure out how to pick up a girl who is not only throwing you an overt pass but who is also obviously a nymphomaniac, then you may as well forget about having sex altogether and sign up for a macrame class instead. Once you've completed the pick-up, the next crucial step is to transport the lucky girl to some romantic spot, either her place or yours. Hers is preferable, since it'll be a little awkward later on, after you're all done, to jump out of bed, put on your clothes, and bid her a suave farewell, if you're in your own house. Motels often prove to be a judicious and manly compromise. Once this stage has been reached, you may proceed to have sex.

As we've already said, no sexual instruction should be necessary for anyone who purports to be a man. Still, there are a couple of small matters that need to be clarified here. First, though birth control is something that should be left entirely up to the woman (if she wants to have a baby, that's her business), it's acceptable for a man to wear a prophylactic during lovemaking, provided that it is the no-frills variety: white, unlubricated, and made in the U.S.A. Any other kind—multicolored or equipped with little doodads—is strictly for degenerates and foreigners. Second, while men are often accused of performing sex in a mechanical "wham-bam-thank-you-Ma'am" fashion, this modus operandi has, in actuality, very little to do with true comportment under the covers. A real man will go to any lengths to whip his partner into a sexual frenzy, provided he does not use any practice or assume any position that is in any way suggestive of passivity or submission. A real man, in short, will never find himself lying on his back during sex and never, *never* do anything that requires him to get on his knees. Remember, a man's got other things to consider than mere pleasure. After all, what if some private detective is taking snap shots of you through a two-way mirror or a peep hole in the motel room wall? How are you going to look then? Not too good, right? And even if there's no one watching, a man still has to live with himself.

After you feel you have performed sex to everyone's satisfaction, you may want to exercise the manly option of leaving immediately. A playful slap on the backside (hers) and a jaunty, devil-may-care "So long, doll" as you walk out the door are guaranteed to make the most manly impression on any woman worth the trouble. As a matter of convenience, however—particularly if it's below freezing outside and the landlord hasn't turned the heat on in your apartment yet—you may want to stay put and postpone leaving, in which case you should memorize some manful pointers about morning-after comportment.

Because, as we have seen, courtesy is an integral component of true manly comportment, a man should always offer to take the female out to breakfast on the morning after. Over the scrambled eggs and ketchup, you may take the opportunity to show her what a heck of a guy you are by asking thoughtful questions about her personal life: where does she come from, is she married,

ON TARGET

Few women can resist a man when he begins putting on the moves in earnest.

LADY KILLER

Women like their men rugged, but a little bit of suavity never hurts. Once you've escorted a skirt back to your pad, you will find it in your best interests to turn on the charm.

does she have a last name, how many men has she slept with. Endearing behavior of this kind will soften the girl up for the final, morning-after brush that will insure a return engagement in the future, if you ever happen to be in the mood. As soon as the breakfast check is paid, simply say, "Make yourself scarce, babe. I'm a busy man." You then get up, turn around, and walk away. But just as it looks as though you're going to take off without another word, you glance back at her over your shoulder, smile mysteriously, and say, "Maybe I'll give you a call sometime." This last line should only be used, however, if you are absolutely certain that you have at no time asked for her number. Just because you're a nice guy doesn't mean you have to let her make unreasonable demands on you. And anyway, it wouldn't be fair to let her get her hopes up *too* high.

A CAUTIONARY WORD ABOUT A SERIOUS SUBJECT

Though hardcore Marxist lesbian feminists frequently claim that all men are, at heart, rapists, the fact is that physical abuse of women is something that only psychos, creeps, and commies indulge in. (Saying horrible, unforgivable things to them is another matter.) While a real man is always the initiator of and aggressor during lovemaking and will on no account ever display any sign of sexual passivity or, for that matter, pleasure, he has no need to use physical force against women to obtain sexual favors, since, as even a casual glance at any Mickey Spillane novel proves, a wide assortment of dolls will constantly be flinging themselves at his feet. In fact, the only time he may be compelled to raise a hand against women is when their sexual demands on him become so importunate and time-consuming that he must beat them off like so many sex-crazed moths drawn by the flaming torch of his manly charisma, or when, as so often happens, a stacked, blonde nympho he's picked up turns out to be either a homicidal, man-hating maniac or a commie spy and must be dispatched with a .45 slug aimed approximately two inches directly below her navel.

MANLY READING COMPREHENSION TEST

Carefully read over the following passage from the conclusion of Dashiell Hammett's classic detective novel, *The Maltese Falcon*. Hammett's hard-boiled hero, Sam Spade, is explaining to Brigid O'Shaughnessy, the woman he loves, why he must send her up the river. There is an important manly message contained in this selection. See if you can figure out what it is.

Brigid O'Shaughnessy blinked her tears away. . . . "You called me a liar," she said. "Now you are lying. You're lying if you say you don't know down in your heart that, in spite of anything I've done, I love you."

Blood streaked Spade's eyeballs now and his long-held smile had become a frightful grimace. He cleared his throat huskily and said: "Making speeches is no damned good now." He put a hand on her shoulder. The hand shook and

jerked. "I don't care who loves who. I'm not going to play the sap for you."

She put a hand on his hand on her shoulder. "Don't help me then," she whispered, "but don't hurt me. Let me go away now."

"No," he said. "I'm sunk if I haven't got you to hand over to the police when they come. That's the only thing that can keep me from going down with the others."

"You won't do that for me?"

"I won't play the sap for you."

"You're not serious," she said. "You don't expect me to think that these things you're saying are sufficient reason for sending me to the—"

"Wait till I'm through and then you can talk. . . . I've no reason in God's world to think that I can trust you and if I did this and got away with it you'd have something on me that you could use whenever you happened to want to. . . . Now on the other side we've got what? All we've got is the fact that maybe you love me and maybe I love you."

"You know," she whispered, "whether you do or not."

"I don't. It's easy enough to be nuts about you." He looked hungrily from her hair to her feet and up to her eyes again. "But I don't know what that amounts to. Does anybody ever? But suppose I do? What of it? Maybe next month I won't. . . . Then what? Then I'll think I played the sap. And if I did it and got sent over then I'd be sure I was the sap."

She put her face up to his face. Her mouth was slightly open with lips a little thrust out. She whispered: "If you loved me you'd need nothing more on that side."

Spade set the edges of his teeth together and said through them: "I won't play the sap for you."

Answer: **The message contained in this passage is: Men don't play the sap for women.**

DECORATING YOUR PAD

How should a man decorate his house or apartment? First of all, he shouldn't. Decorating is woman's work. But in those cases when a woman is not immediately available (you can rarely find one when you need one; that's just the way they are), it is perfectly all right for a man to step into the breach because, when you come right down to it, a man should never have to depend on a woman. If he has some handy Man's Woman hanging around the place anyway—a doll with an appreciation for Naugahyde upholstery and coat racks made out of moose antlers—then fine: let her have a crack at it. Under no circumstances, however, should he turn to or even ask the advice of a Woman-in-Man's-Clothing, much as this type seems to enjoy interior decoration. A man should either get another man to do the job or rely on his own rugged self. Having settled this issue decisively, he should proceed with a manly eye for decorative detail. Such perception can usually be attained by polishing off a case of Schlitz.

For the man who has already arrived financially, the procedure for fixing up his home is relatively simple. The furniture should consist of overstuffed

BACHELOR QUARTERS

A clothesline strung across the middle of the living room will add a touch of distinction to any manly pad.

chairs, upholstered in cowhide, and stained-wood tables on top of which may be placed engraved beer steins and ships-in-a-bottle. The floor should be covered with bear rugs and the walls adorned with rifle racks, Remington prints, stuffed animal heads, and autographed photos of Ted Turner. In general, the room should exude the atmosphere of the Wyoming Stock Growers Association Cheyenne Club, circa 1902. A spray can containing essence-of-cigar smoke may also be used to good effect.

For the average man, who has yet to make it to the top, there are other, less expensive ways of gussying up his home that will produce highly desirable results. Indeed, certain authorities in our field maintain that decorating a home in the cheapest possible manner is often the more comportmental option, since a luxurious living space is not high on any list of manly priorities. Mike Hammer doesn't exactly spend a lot of time moping around his apartment, wishing he had enough money to buy a new six-piece living room suite. A man shouldn't require anything more in the way of comfort than can be found in the average army barracks, locker room, or jail cell. If a bunk bed, bare light bulb, water basin, and toilet bowl were good enough for G. Gordon Liddy, they should be good enough for you. Thus, even the wealthy man may prefer to forego the luxury he can easily afford and stick close to the following guidelines.

First and most important, the reader should maintain constant vigilance against the infiltration of any plant into his living area. Plants are close cousins to flowers, and we all know what kind of individual likes flowers. Second, a man would be well advised to buy at least one sofa for the living room (an old army cot decked out with a few wet-look vinyl bolsters will serve), since he is bound to find it difficult to put the moves on his date while they are perched on his weightlifter's bench or on one of the discarded bar stools he has cleverly converted into chairs.

The rest of the living room may be furnished with milk crates and cable spools. Lamps will come in handy, but lampshades may be dispensed with. They just cut down on the light and otherwise get in the way. With a bit of imagination, the reader can easily construct handsome table lamps out of empty bottles of Colt .45 Malt Liquor. As for maintenance, the reader may want to keep a broom around so he can sweep the place out every couple of months whether it needs it or not. In between sweepings, a man can put the excess dust balls to good use by arranging them artistically in the corner to simulate the topographical layout of the Ardennes during the Battle of the Bulge. The finishing touch to the room can be supplied by tacking up *Hustler* centerfolds and reproduction paintings of bulldogs in green visors playing poker.

Additional decorative flourishes may be introduced as the man sees fit, but an appropriately virile home should include all of the above elements. By decorating in this manner, the reader will be able to create a manly abode that is visually appealing as well as functional. In every quadrant, from the curtainless windows to the caked-up soap dish to the sleeping bag laid out smartly on the cot, the casual observer will readily see that here lives a man, not a woman. You have now found your home.

PHOTO QUIZ #2

WHAT'S WRONG WITH THIS PICTURE?

Above is a prime example of a manly pad. Note the tasteful and ingenious designer details: the vinyl bean bag easy chair, the motorcycle tire converted into a daring piece of post-modernist art, the spare engine parts cleverly used to prop up the furniture. Everything is perfecto—except for one, glaring flaw. Can you find what is wrong with this picture?

Answer: What is wrong with this picture is that it shows a male behind a vacuum cleaner. Obviously, in spite of the athletic-type shirt he's wearing, he can't possibly be the inhabitant of such a thoroughly manly domicile (his sandals are another giveaway). He must be the cleaning lady.

MANLY CUISINE: THE 60-SECOND GOURMET

Even though he has no full-time woman to cook for him, the single man must nevertheless eat. Exhaustive laboratory-controlled experiments performed during the preparation of this book proved conclusively that the prolonged absence of food in even the most manly of individuals produced marked symptoms of womanly behavior, including fainting spells, extreme languor, and, in some cases, an embarrassing tendency to lapse into coma. Further study indicated that, particularly in the latter instance, the subject was capable of performing alarmingly few manly acts. The conclusion drawn by our crack team of researchers was clear and uncompromising: Men must eat.

Ideally, the single man should always eat out, either in a greasy spoon, a corner bar, a roadside diner, or the Playboy Club. But a man should not limit himself in this regard. It is understandable that any hombre worth his salt would look warily upon the kitchen as a veritable no-man's-land fraught with womanly peril. But the reader shouldn't allow himself to be intimidated. When the situation demands it, he should be able to hitch up his pants, stick out his chest, and march right into that kitchen, ready to go one-on-one with any cooking utensil that gets in his way. Look at it like this: if a woman can do it, it's got to be a breeze for a man. He may not like it, but a man's gotta do what a man's gotta do. If he's got what it takes, he should be able to lug out the frying pan, slap on some grease, and throw in a mound of ground beef, unafraid and undaunted. Of course, if he doesn't have any ground beef around, he better get the hell out of there and

RECOMMENDED DISHES

FRIED PORK RINDS (EASY TO PREPARE AND MIGHTY GOOD EATIN')

PIZZA WITH ANCHOVIES

LUNCH MEAT

BEEF JERKY

TACOS

BEER NUTS

BLOOD-RED STEAK

ARTIFICIAL ADDITIVES

DINTY MOORE BEEF STEW (GREAT ON A COOKOUT)

SPAM (GREAT ANYWHERE)

SCRAMBLED EGGS WITH KETCHUP

haul ass over to the neighborhood oyster bar pronto.

Regardless of whether he puts on the feed-bag at the lunch counter or brasses it out in the kitchen, the reader should choose his food with the utmost care. Certain meals will feed the comportmental juices just as surely as others will render you permanently impotent. To paraphrase a great proverb: The way to the manly heart is through the stomach, and the passage to that stomach should be closely guarded. Provided here is an invaluable guide to the kinds of food that will keep a man manly and those that will sap his strength, energy, and will to live, and turn him into a woman.

> ***He likes people. You can never count on a man like that.***
>
> **Burt Lancaster in the movie *Vera Cruz.***

UNMANLY FOODS TO BE AVOIDED AT ALL COST

PART THREE

MAN AT WORK AND PLAY

MANLY OCCUPATIONS

There is one component of a man's life without which he has no reason to live, something that defines the parameters and meaning of his very existence. That necessary ingredient is, of course, a job. In a very real sense, a man *is* his job. Without a back-breaking occupation to call his own, a man goes soft and turns into a quivering, gutless mass of female jello. A man cannot comport himself unless he has put in his eight hours-plus a day, five days-plus a week. If he has no job, he is liable to stay home and, if he's careless, even wander into the kitchen, the first fatal step on the downward path into utter degradation. If for no other reason, a man should go to work so he won't have to watch the Phil Donahue show.

Before any of you out there starts feeling smug and saying to yourself, "Well, I guess I'm in the clear; I've got a job," let's get one thing straight right away. It's not enough simply to go out to work in the morning. You must have a *job* in the full manly sense of the word. You must pursue an occupation that demands complete, 100-proof comportment every single hour of every single working day. The importance of a man's choice of career cannot be over-

RECOMMENDED MANLY OCCUPATIONS

STEAM FITTER
LUMBER YARD FOREMAN
HIT MAN
TRUCK DRIVER
LONGSHOREMAN
TWO-FISTED CUTTHROAT EXECUTIVE
FORKLIFT OPERATOR
GLOBE-TROTTING MERCENARY
CONSTRUCTION WORKER
CHARACTER ACTOR IN SAM PECKINPAH MOVIES
RODEO RIDER
AUTO MECHANIC
MOUNTAIN MAN
DIRECTOR OF LIGHT BEER COMMERCIALS
COP
FIREMAN
HOCKEY PLAYER
BOUNTY HUNTER
STUNT PILOT
BUTCHER
ROUSTABOUT
SADISTIC PRISON GUARD
BARTENDER
S.W.A.T. TEAM COMMANDER
BLACKSMITH
DRILL SERGEANT
ALCOHOLIC AUTHOR WHO LIKES TO HUNT

emphasized. To put it simply, in order to be a man, one has to work like a man. And if that's too hard for you to "relate to," hoss, then why don't you just stay home and knit yourself a sweater? Either that or go back to Vladivostok where you belong.

> ***It may be a lousy war, but it's the only war we've got.***
>
> **Marine Corps General "Chesty" Puller, referring to Korea.**

Obviously a decision of such overwhelming importance requires some heavy-duty thinking. Or at least it used to. Now, with the publication of this book, in which we list every possible vocation suitable for a man, thinking becomes superfluous, which is the way it should be. There's no reason for a man to sit around scratching his head any more than he has to. We've got academic eggheads to handle that sort of thing, and they're welcome to it. One of the great pleasures of being a man is that you can just go ahead and do something without engaging in the tedious, not to say emasculating, process of actually having to think about it.

From this moment on, finding a job will be a simple matter of reading over the following recommendations and picking the one that appeals to you most. This list has been carefully researched and includes only those jobs that will allow a man to comport himself as he sees fit.

Any individual with even a modicum of manliness in him should find that the above list contains more than enough options for a fulfilling career. We are aware, of course, that today's job market is tight and

> ***Man for the field and woman for the hearth:***
> ***Man for the sword and for the needle she:***
> ***Man with the head and woman with the heart:***
> ***Man to command and woman to obey:***
> ***All else confusion.***
>
> **Alfred, Lord Tennyson *The Princess***

that a well-meaning individual may have pored over this list and carefully made his first and alternative choices, only to find that these positions are unavailable at present. (Naturally, if you comport yourself during your job search in the approved manly manner, then the mere nonexistence of the job should represent only a minor obstacle.) During this regrettable interim, you may be forced to accept temporary employment of a not entirely virile nature. As demeaning as this may be, the reader should be man enough to keep a stiff upper lip and bull his way through until things take a turn for the better. There are, however, certain jobs that you should not even think about taking, regardless of how dire your financial situation is. Compared to these occupations, staying home and watching "The Galloping Gourmet" is a manful pursuit. To keep you from ending up in one of these compromising positions, we have provided the following list. Study it carefully and never let it out of your mind.

JOBS NO MAN SHOULD EVER BE CAUGHT DEAD DOING

CHOREOGRAPHER
OWNER OF A NATURAL FOOD STORE
VILLAGE VOICE EDITOR
MUSICOLOGIST
MALE NURSE
SEX SLAVE FOR AGING FEMALE PATRON
FLORIST
WAITER IN A FRENCH RESTAURANT
MIME
CUISINART SALESMAN

IDENTIFY THE MANLY WORLD LEADER

Pictured below are four famous politicians, one of whom is a man. Who is this manly world leader?

Sorry, there was no room for the answer.

MANLY RECREATION

A man must work but he must also play, and with equal dedication to the time-honored principles of comportment. Indeed, manly recreation may even be more important than a job, since it is during his leisure hours that a man generally achieves his highest level of pure gusto. The way in which you have fun, then, is crucial to your standing in the manly community. Some pastimes are obvious—taking in a ball game, duck hunting, tying a tin can to a stray dog's tail and watching him run himself to death—but others are a bit more arcane. For this reason, we are provid-

Why shouldn't I play? There was no blood and the bone wasn't sticking out.

Jack Youngblood, defensive end for the Los Angeles Rams, in response to a reporter who asked why he took part in two N.F.L. playoff games with a fractured leg.

A MANLY DAY AT THE BEACH

ELEPHANT WALK

Balancing oneself on the head of a charging bull elephant is a manly recreational activity favored by those in the know.

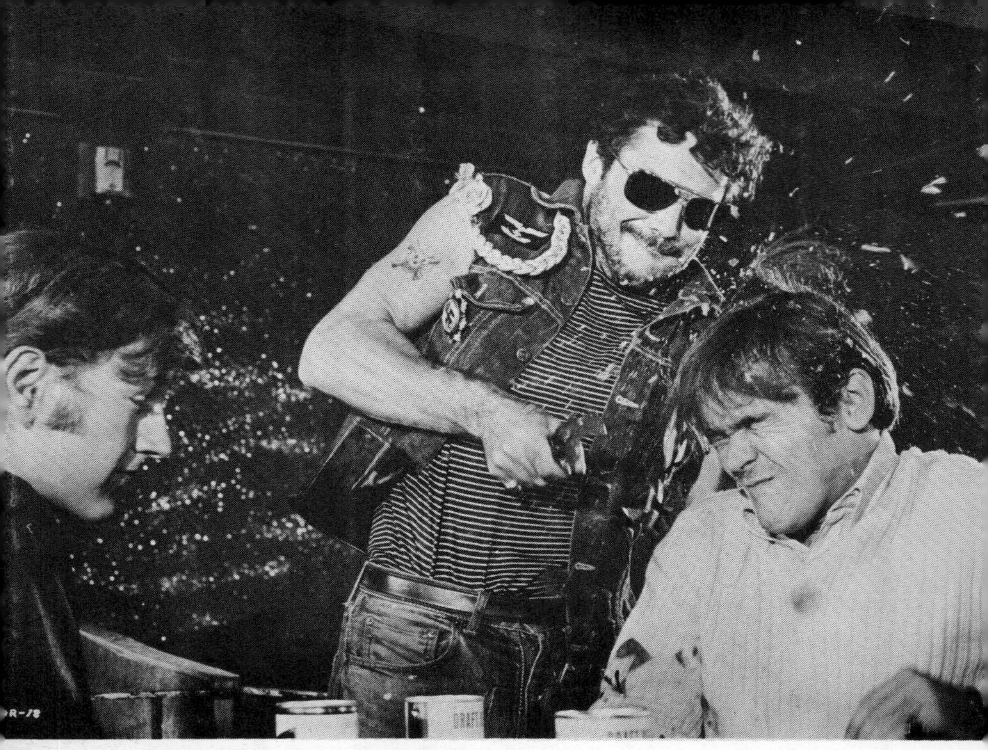

MEN HAVING FUN

Big Frank from Frisco is a black belt in karate who goes into any fight with the idea of jerking people's eyeballs out of their sockets. It is a traditional karate move and not difficult for anyone who knows what he's doing . . . "You don't really jerk out the eyeball," Big Frank explained. "You just sorta spring it, so it pops outta the socket."

Hunter S. Thompson, *Hell's Angels*

Dwight White, one of the defensive linemen for the Pittsburgh Steelers, was once described in a Cleveland newspaper as an individual who accepted the Three Stooges on TV with such credulity that, when he finally learned the slapstick comics weren't really hitting each other, he got so mad that, to express himself, he went out and set a cat on fire.

William Barry Furlong, "Football Violence"

PLAYING THE GAME

When you're looking for a good way to spend your leisure time, try to find an activity that is both relaxing and rewarding.

ing the following convenient list of virile recreational activities for the man who is determined to have fun no matter what the cost in either financial or human terms. When your local theater is not holding a "Spend the Day with Clint Eastwood" film festival or when the televised "Texas Death" pro wrestling match has been preempted for a John Denver "Save the Whales" benefit concert, simply consult the following list for good ways to fill up your spare time.

1 Set up a row of sixteen Volkswagens at the lip of the Grand Canyon. Approach the line of cars on a customized, jet-propelled motorcycle, zoom up and off an up-tilted ramp, and soar along the top of the cars with the intention of landing safely on the opposite side of the canyon. There is absolutely no chance of coming out of this thing alive, but if you're a man, you can take it.

2 Kick down all the doors in your house.

3 Dive off the top of the World Trade Center into a trampoline on the street below.

4 Get a friend (preferably one you never liked very much anyway) to drive full speed down a single-lane road while you drive straight at him from the opposite direction, and see who chickens out first.

5 Fight a war in Angola.

6 Drink straight tequila until you can't see, then go over to your neighbor's house and puke on his car.

7 Stick a wet hand in a live toaster. Repeat.

8 Convince the wife to take up belly dancing.

9 Take a midnight stroll through the South Bronx unarmed.

10 Go bowling.

MANLY VACATIONS

Two weeks of hunting grizzlies with a crossbow in the Alaskan wilderness

Shark fishing in the Florida Keys

A ten-day gambling and whoring junket in Vegas

Hang-gliding through enemy air space

Canoe trip down white water during which you and your companions are attacked by depraved hillbillies

Wild boar hunting in Afghanistan

Travelling to Berlin as a CIA courier under the guise of a tourist from Lafayette, Indiana

Ten nights in a barroom

MANLY EXTRA
THE MANLY WAY TO START THE DAY

MANLY MOVIES

Sands of Iwo Jima (1949)
Stars John Wayne as Sgt. Stryker, the type of guy who'd give you a square deal even when he's pounding in your teeth with a rifle butt. Highly recommended for children to teach them the facts of life.

Hercules and the Captive Women (1963, Italian)
What can we say about Hercules that hasn't been said before? Just an all-around heck of a guy.

Dirty Harry (1971)
Clint Eastwood as the embodiment of everything good about America: morality, justice, and large caliber handguns.

Dawn of the Dead (1979)
Two hours of zombies getting their heads blown off by S.W.A.T. officers. Not a think-picture, just something to relax with and enjoy.

Kiss Me Deadly (1955)
A gutter-tough Mickey Spillane mystery that makes *The Maltese Falcon* look like a Girl Scout jamboree.

Death Wish (1974)
Charles Bronson in his greatest role as a conscientious objector who decides to become a man.

Petrified Forest (1936)
Humphrey Bogart as Duke Mantee, a hard-bitten, homicidal fugitive who whips a dinerfull of namby-pambies into line. Unfortunately, the film is somewhat marred by the presence of known ladies-man Leslie Howard, who spends most of the time yakking away about poetry, alienation, and other homosexual topics. Apparently growing tired of listening to himself talk, Howard ultimately asks Duke Mantee to shoot him in the chest. Fortunately, Duke is an obliging guy.

Paint Your Wagon (1969)
Starring Clint Eastwood and Lee Marvin. The only manly musical ever made (though *Guys and Dolls*, starring Marlon Brando and Frank Sinatra, comes close to qualifying).

The Green Berets (1967)
John Wayne tells the truth about Vietnam.

Raging Bull (1980)
Robert DeNiro as Jake LaMotta, a person to admire.

Some director once told Mitchum at the start of a picture, "I've got a hot temper. When I get rattled, I shout at actors. But don't let it worry you—next day I've forgotten all about it." Mitchum said he understood—"I've got a temper, too. When a director yells at me, I flatten him."

Grover Lewis, "Robert Mitchum: Last of the Celluloid Desperadoes"

Any movie starring Robert Mitchum.

The Dogs of War (1981)
A moving, sensitive portrait of the globe-trotting mercenary, a breed of man that's been getting a lot of bad press lately from the Eastern liberal media conspiracy. This film is also notable for its moving, sensitive attitude towards women, as when one of the mercenaries explains that he would rather sign on for a bloody commando raid on a West African nation than hang around home with his pregnant wife because "watching her get fat is gonna be nauseating."

Six-Gun Trail (1939)
A Western starring Colonel Tim McCoy, from back when they made cowboy movies that a man could sink his teeth into, before they had to gussy them up with psychology, national guilt, characterization, and what have you.

Texas Chainsaw Massacre (1974)
Anyone can use a chainsaw to cut logs for the fireplace, but it takes a real man to use one as a hand weapon. Fun for the whole family.

Bring Me the Head of Alfredo Garcia (1974)
Directed by Sam "The Man" Peckinpah. Title says it all.

Hell's Angels on Wheels (1967)
An early Jack Nicholson feature about one of the most misunderstood bunch of stand-up guys in the country.

Hondo (1953)
A 3-D Western starring John Wayne. The Duke comin' right at ya off the screen—what more could you ask from a movie?

Ralph Meeker as Mike Hammer in the movie *Kiss Me Deadly* shows a young punk how to take it like a man.

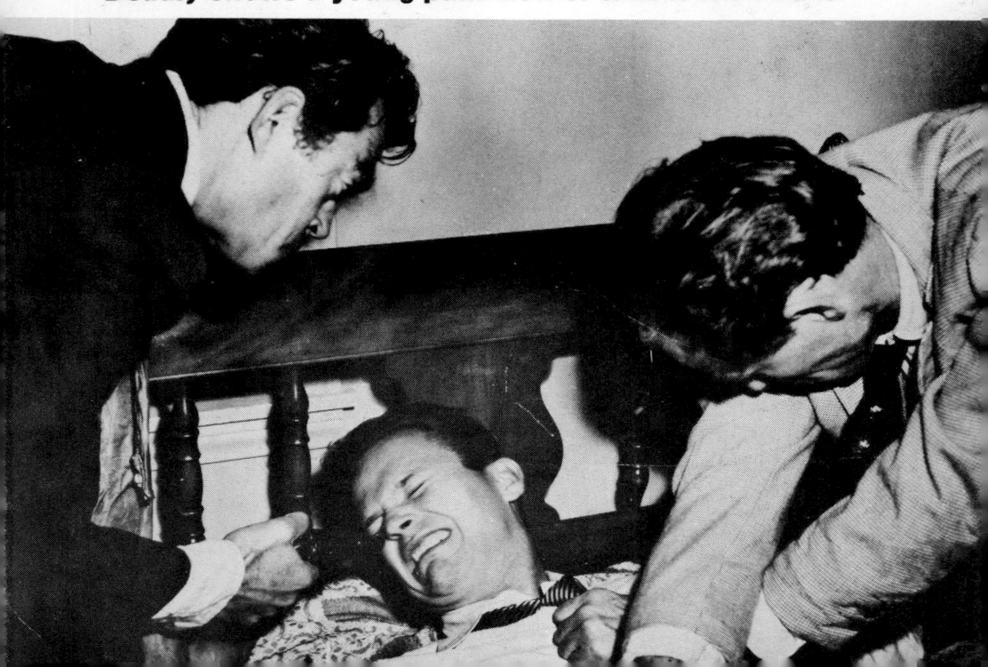

MANLY SONGS

By its very nature, music is not very manly, although it can on occasion seem manly when you're listening to it over a jukebox as you guzzle liquor in your local gin mill. But boozy impressions notwithstanding, the hard fact is that, for the most part, men just don't sing. For this reason it is easier to find examples of manly instrumental music than manly songs. Any number of John Philip Sousa marches are candidates for comportmental immortality, for instance, as are the soundtracks to such movies as *The Magnificent Seven* and John Wayne's cinematic masterpiece, *The Alamo*. And no one in his right mind would deny that "Hawaii Five-O" by the Ventures is one of the great artistic achievements of Western man.

Still and all, there have been a number of exceptional individuals who have infiltrated the womanly profession of singing with highly comportmental results. They're a rare breed of man, however, and their output has been necessarily limited. The following are, in fact, the only manly songs ever recorded.

"I'm a Man"
by the Spencer Davis Group

"500% More Man"
by Bo Diddley

Anything ever recorded
by Waylon Jennings

"Walk like a Man"
by the Four Seasons

(A controversial choice, since singing in a high-pitched, nasal falsetto is not, as a rule, considered very manly. The lyrics are so powerful, however, that they more than compensate for the rather questionable vocal style affected by the otherwise virile lead singer.)

"Ballad of the Green Berets"
by Lt. Barry Sadler

"Hot Rod Lincoln"
by Johnny Bond

"Stand by Your Man"
by Tammy Wynette ***(a Man's Woman if ever there was one)***

"The Fightin' Side of Me"
by Merle Haggard

"Little GTO"
by the Hondells

"Convoy"
by C. W. McCall

Anything ever recorded by Willie Nelson ***(with the possible exception of "Somewhere Over the Rainbow")***

"Folsom Prison Blues"
by Johnny Cash

"Ballad of Lt. Calley"
by Tex Ritter

"Deadman's Curve"
by Jan and Dean

"Great Balls of Fire"
by Jerry Lee Lewis

MANLY DANCES

1. ______________________________

2. ______________________________

3. ______________________________

4. ______________________________

5. ______________________________

6. ______________________________

7. ______________________________

8. ______________________________

9. ______________________________

10. ______________________________

MANLY READING

With the exception of car repair manuals, gun catalogues, and the collected works of Mickey Spillane, books are written for women. Still, it is possible that, on certain rare occasions, a man may find himself stuck at home in the evening with nothing on TV but "Masterpiece Theater," a news documentary on food additives, and a rerun of "Little House on the Prairie." If the latest issue of *Popular Mechanics* hasn't arrived yet in the mail, he may be tempted, out of desperation, to pick up the literary classic he spots lying among his kid's schoolbooks. This chapter will give the reader helpful tips on which books will provide an acceptable few hours of manly entertainment and which are a complete waste of time.

It is important to keep in mind that you cannot judge a book by its title. The unwary reader, for example, is likely to think that *The American* is worth glancing at unless he realizes that Henry James, like his pal George Eliot, was not a man. Even works by manly authors can sometimes have deliberately misleading titles. "The Killers" by Ernest Hemingway, for instance, is generally acknowledged to be one of the dullest and most dishonest stories ever written, since no one even gets killed in it.

The following are some high-toned books which can be safely recommended to the manly reader with an hour or two to kill.

The Deerslayer by James Fenimore Cooper. Readers may be disappointed at first to find that this is not a manual on the manly art of shooting deer and put off by the long and pointless descriptive passages (which can easily be skipped). Still, perseverance will pay off, since this novel does contain a number of satisfying scenes of good old-fashioned frontier violence and a hero who kills lots of people, though he ruins the effect somewhat by being unnecessarily apologetic about it.

Adventures of Huckleberry Finn by Mark Twain. While this is generally regarded as a children's book, it contains several manful episodes, such as a bloody feud in which virtually all the members of two families

TREASURE CHEST

Considered by many to be the single most manly publication in history, this exceptionally rare issue of *Man's Action* magazine (Vol. I, No. 11, Nov. 1959) has reportedly commanded prices of up to $8000 at men's conventions in Buffalo and Oil City . . .

. . . A look at the Contents, with such articles as "They Forced Me to Belly Dance on the Sahara" and "I Fought the Commie White Slavers," explains why this volume is so coveted by men everywhere.

CONTENTS

succeed in wiping each other out and a stirring shootout in which a Southern gentleman named Sherbirn guns down an unarmed drunk and then proceeds to make a very manly speech to the mob that assembles to lynch him.

The Red Badge of Courage by Stephen Crane. The heartwarming story of a dirty, sniveling little coward who runs away from a battle but then shapes up, learns how to fight like a man, and is honored with the award referred to in the title.

Sanctuary by William Faulkner. Lots of manly doings here if you can figure out what the hell the author is talking about, which you probably won't be able to half the time. For some mysterious reason, Faulkner had a hard time saying anything straight, though in all other respects he was a good ole boy, and in this novel he has created a fun-loving, exemplary hero named Popeye who knows how to show a girl a good time.

The Iliad by Homer. Though this book was not written by an American, it does contain numerous scenes of manly action and bloodshed that are surprisingly advanced, considering how long ago this book was written. ("But before this Achilles took his life with the sword from close up/ for he struck him in the belly next the navel, and all his guts poured/ out on the ground.")

Tamburlaine the Great by Christopher Marlowe. A literary curiosity. Though the author of this play was a real man who died a man's death, getting stabbed through the eye in a barroom brawl, he chose, for some unknown reason, to write this book in poetry, which of course is something that no man would ever choose to read, let alone write. Still, the hero proves himself repeatedly to be a man, as for example on those frequent occasions when he lays siege to various towns and slaughters all the inhabitants. Worth a look.

No American writer should write like an Englishman, or a Frenchman; let him write like a man, for then he will be sure to write like an American.

Herman Melville

THE TEN GREATEST MANLY AMERICAN BOOKS

1. I, the Jury
by Mickey Spillane

2. My Gun is Quick
by Mickey Spillane

3. The Virginian
by Owen Wister

4. Death in the Afternoon
by Ernest Hemingway

5. Deliverance
by James Dickey

6. The Big Kill
by Mickey Spillane

7. Will
by G. Gordon Liddy

8. An American Dream
by Norman Mailer

9. Me, Hood
by Mickey Spillane

10. The Girl Hunters
by Mickey Spillane

THE WIT AND WISDOM OF G. GORDON LIDDY

ON THE CORRECT WAY OF LEARNING HOW TO SWIM

"... during my second year at summer camp, I learned to swim by the simple expedient of being taken out in a rowboat to the middle of the lake by older boys who told me I was to be thrown overboard. I was expected to plead for mercy and carry on. I did neither.... I was thrown overboard when I refused to beg and, to my own surprise, promptly swam all the way to shore. When other boys were taken on the rowboat ride, I felt contempt for those who whimpered."

ON WHAT TO LOOK FOR IN A WIFE

"I had another and more difficult decision to make at that time—whether to ask a certain young lady to 'wait for' me. I was enamored of her, yet something held me back from full commitment. . . . The young woman was intelligent and beautiful, but I wanted more mathematical ability in the gene pool from which my children would spring. I also wanted size—height and heavy bone structure so that my children would be physically as well as intellectually powerful—and she was of less than average height with thin, delicate bones. . . . I did not ask her to wait for me and we parted friends. Somewhere, I felt sure, I would find the woman I wanted to bear my children: a highly intelligent, tall, fair, powerfully built Teuton, whose mind worked like . . . the electronic computer."

ON HOW TO CARE FOR A WIFE

"We *still* wanted six children; but it made no sense to damage Fran's health and lessen her ability to participate in their raising as well as procreation by having all six within six years. Although one of the reasons I had chosen Frances to be the mother of my children was her size and strength, which should have enabled her to bear half a dozen high-performance children, I certainly had not intended to risk damage by pushing her to design limit."

ON RELIGION

"Common sense tells us that minor problems require and justify but minor responses, and only extreme problems require and justify extreme solutions. In the case of killing it is well to remember that the Ten Commandments, translated correctly from the original Aramaic, do not contain the injunction 'Thou shalt not kill.' It reads, 'Thou shalt not do murder.' Quite another thing."

(All passages from *Will*.)

Mike Hammer drinks beer instead of cognac because I can't spell cognac.

Mickey Spillane, speaking at a meeting of the Mystery Writers of America

GUESS THE AUTHOR

Instructions: Reprinted below are quotes from world-famous literature. Read each passage carefully and see if you can identify the manly author who wrote it.

1. Call me Ishmael.

2. I snapped the side of the rod across his jaw and laid the flesh open to the bone. He dropped the sap and staggered into the big boy with a scream. I pounded his teeth back into his mouth with the end of the barrel, and I took my own damn time about kicking him in the face.

3. A man can be destroyed but not defeated.

4. There was no sense to busting my hand on his skull, so I lashed out with my foot and the toe of my shoe caught the guy right in the face. He toppled over sideways, still running, and collapsed against the wall. His lower teeth were protruding through his lip. Two of his incisors were lying beside his nose, plastered there with blood.

5. A true man belongs to no other time or place, but is the centre of things.

6. I swung on him with all of my hundred and ninety pounds. My fist went up to the wrist in his stomach. He flopped to the floor vomiting his lungs out, his face turning gradually purple.

Answers:

1. Herman Melville, *Moby-Dick*
2. Mickey Spillane, *The Big Kill*
3. Ernest Hemingway, *The Old Man and the Sea*
4. Mickey Spillane, *I, the Jury*
5. Ralph Waldo Emerson, "Self-Reliance"
6. Mickey Spillane, *I, the Jury*

MANLY BONUS

THE MANLY WAY
TO ASK FOR
A RAISE

FIND THE MANLY PET

The art department lost the correct answer.

Pet ownership can certainly be manly, although, like everything else in life, it has to be handled correctly. Certain pets, such as tropical fish, hamsters, and canaries were obviously devised for the pantyhose set, while others—tarantulas, boa constrictors, moray eel, piranha—were just as obviously put on earth to provide companionship for men. Cats are strictly for women, dogs for men. Not every canine, however, is worthy of being a man's best friend. Only one of the dogs in these pictures, for instance, can be considered manly. Can you find him?

THE MOST IMPORTANT PERSON IN YOUR LIFE: YOUR CAR

A man without a car is like a cowboy without a horse. Bodily parts and concealed handguns aside, the car is a man's most important tool of manly comportment. Without it, he is a mere fragment of manliness, unable to mobilize the diverse elements of his life into one cohesive, virile entity. The truth of this should be self-evident. But for the benefit of those whimpering skeptics out there, we are prepared to offer hard, irrefutable proof. Just look at New York City and San Francisco, the principal hotbeds of womanliness in our nation today. Why do you think these once great cities of ours seem to have jettisoned manliness entirely? It couldn't be because the people who live there depend mostly on public transportation instead of cars, could it? Well, guess again, pal.

To be a man, you must own a car—this much we know. But exactly what kind of car should you own? The particular make is not important, as long as it's American. A man isn't choosy about that sort of thing, since by the time he's finished working over the engine and customizing approximately seventy percent of the body, nobody's going to recognize the damned thing anyway. Your only concern should be to make sure you acquire a car with a stick shift. A man should never drive an automatic transmission. The automatic transmission, you may remember, was invented so that women could learn how to block traffic from the driver's seat, instead of doing it from the passenger side by jabbering away at hubbie so much he couldn't concentrate. Just take any given traffic jam, weave your way up to the front, and we guarantee that you'll find it all narrows down to some skirt trying to make a right-hand turn from a left-turn lane. Either that or she's making herself up in the rearview mirror. You can check it out for yourself.

Once you've gotten your car, the real fun begins. There's no point at all in investing in an auto if you just plan to take the keys and start driving. You don't know what living is all about unless you keep your machine inside the garage or up on blocks in your backyard for at least half a year, while you overhaul every single part.

Obviously, if you're going to soup up some old heap, it's best for all concerned if you have some idea of what you're doing. If you never learn any-

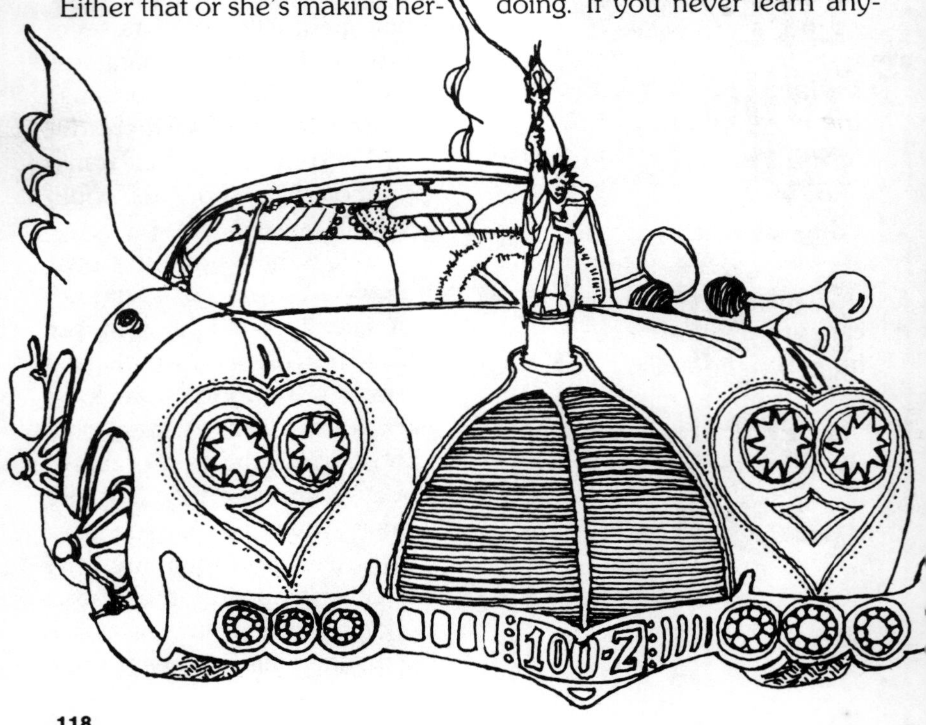

In a few days a general meeting of the militia was called for the purpose of raising volunteers; and when the day arrived for that meeting, my wife, who had heard me say I meant to go to war, began to beg me not to turn out. She said she was a stranger in the parts where we lived, had no connections living near her, and that she and our little children would be left in a lonesome and unhappy situation if I went away. It was mighty hard to go against such arguments as these; but my countrymen had been murdered, and I knew that the next thing would be, that the Indians would be scalping the women and children all about there, if we didn't put a stop to it. I reasoned the case with her as well as I could, and told her, that if every man would wait till his wife got willing for him to go to war, there would be no fighting done, that I was as able to go as any man in the world, and that I believed it was a duty I owed to my country. Whether she was satisfied with this reasoning or not, she did not tell me; but seeing I was bent on it, all she did was to cry a little, and turn about to her work. The truth is, my dander was up, and nothing but war could bring it right again.

The Autobiography of David Crockett

thing else in your life, you should know engines inside-out. And we're not just talking carburetors and spark plugs here. If you don't know a blazer cam from a manifold, then you've got a tough road ahead of you, fella. No man settles for an engine that can't be improved, and if you don't know how to make at least some alterations, then number one on your next Christmas list had better be a year's subscription to *Popular Hot Rodding.* It's vitally important that you be able to work casual references to crankshafts and gaskets into your everyday conversation. When you meet the mailman coming up the drive on Saturday morning, you should be able to tell him that you just fixed up your '68 Plymouth with a .060 overbore to produce 417 CID, added triple-chrome-plated dual exhaust bolt-on sidepipes, and then

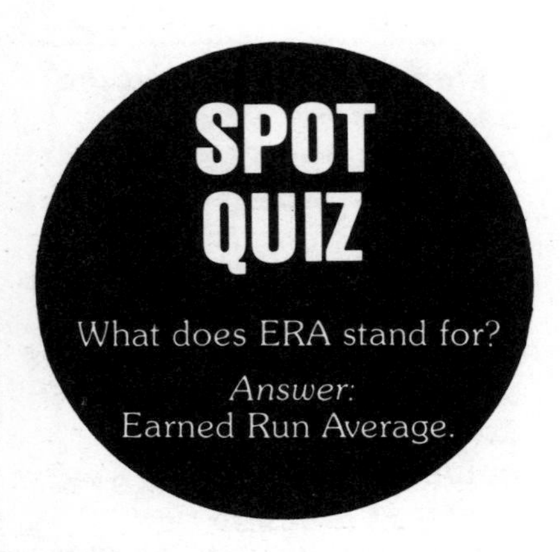

threw in Arias 8-to-1 aluminum blower pistons just for laughs. If that doesn't get a rise out of him, then he must be some kind of liberal. To hell with him.

After you've put the final touches on your little beauty, you might experience a vague sense of depression at the thought that the most important part of your life is over. Not to worry. There's never been an engine built, or even rebuilt, that can't be spruced up a little more. The tinkering need not ever end. And even if no improvements immediately suggest themselves, you can always take your masterpiece out for a late Saturday night spin, wrap it around a telephone pole, and start the whole thing from scratch. Limitless possibilities are available to you. You just have to keep an open mind.

But don't get us wrong. The manly pleasures of owning a car extend beyond mere renovation and maintenance. One of the greatest joys a man can know is simply to hop in his car and tool around, while he feels that raw power purring under the hood. As every man knows, one of the most satisfying forms of dating is to take your girl out for hours upon hours of aimless nighttime driving. There are few women who can resist the charm of such an activity. Still, as profound an experience as this is for all concerned, never forget one thing: under no circumstances should you feel compelled to hunt up some skirt whenever you feel the urge to go joyriding. Cruising all by yourself is a spiritual experience that every man should know. Admittedly, having a delectable dame seated alongside you and growing more wanton with every tight turn you take has a lot to recommend it. But once you swing out onto the highway on a solo mission, you'll find you won't be missing a thing. Remember, when you're in your car, you're never alone. Your air scoop is plenty enough company for you.

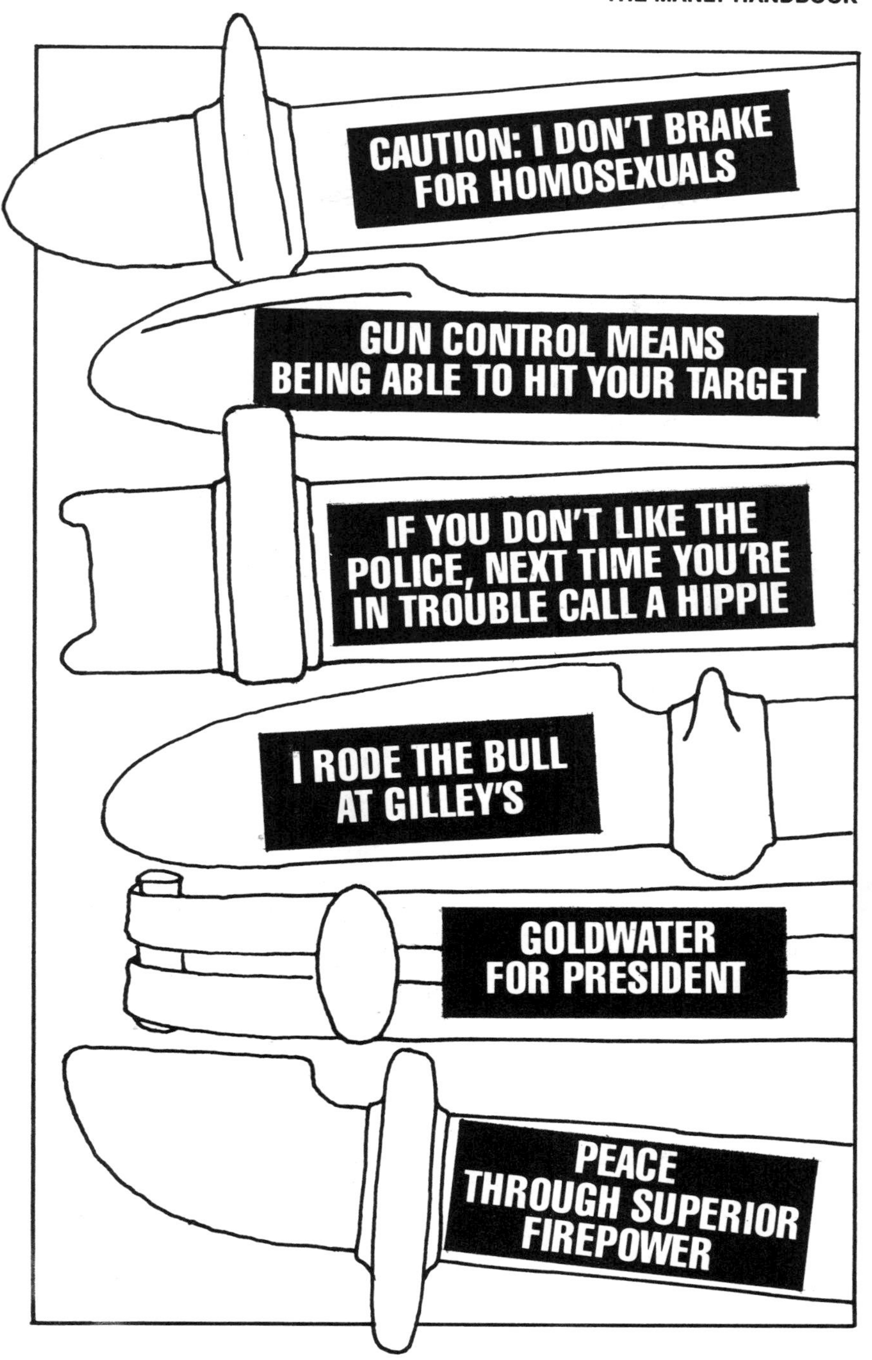
CAUTION: I DON'T BRAKE
FOR HOMOSEXUALS
GUN CONTROL MEANS
BEING ABLE TO HIT YOUR TARGET
IF YOU DON'T LIKE THE
POLICE, NEXT TIME YOU'RE
IN TROUBLE CALL A HIPPIE
I RODE THE BULL
AT GILLEY'S
GOLDWATER
FOR PRESIDENT
PEACE
THROUGH SUPERIOR
FIREPOWER

WHICH MEN ARE HAVING THE MOST FUN?

Study these pictures of people at play, then identify the men who are having the most fun.

The answer to this quiz will not be found anywhere.

PART FOUR

THE DEAD MAN

HOW TO DIE LIKE A MAN

We mentioned at the start of this book that being a man was a "lifelong mission," but actually we understated the case a little bit. Living in a manly way is the most honorable thing you'll ever do, but if you fail to *die* like a man, too, then you've just been wasting your time, as well as ours. You might as well have not gone through all the trouble in the first place.

The trick here is that, after you're gone, you want people to say, "He went out like a man." Let's say, for example, that you're going to be given the chair for some manly infraction. You don't want to go out kicking and screaming. You want to make the last march to the hot seat with an Approved Manly Sneer on your mug, trade quips with the guard who's adjusting the straps, and then, when the switch is thrown, say something like, "Hey, can't you guys turn up the heat a little bit? It's chilly sitting here with my head shaved and my pants legs cut open like this." That way, the boys in the press box are sure to be impressed and say, "He went out like a man."

Another admirable way to make your exit is to be riddled with bullets while engaged in a blazing gun battle, such as you might find outside your neighborhood bank during a holdup or in the midst of a presidential parade. Some helpful tips in this regard: You should make a point of saying something pithy as you go under, like "This is funny," or "Is this the end of Rico?" or "Give me a beer." If no words come to mind at the critical moment, simply grab an American flag and press it to your chest. (This is just one of many reasons why it's a good idea to carry a flag with you at all times.)

Combat had its own finite series of tests, and one of the greatest sins was "chattering" or "jabbering" on the radio. The combat frequency was to be kept clear of all but strategically essential messages, and all unenlightening comments were regarded as evidence of funk, of the wrong stuff. A Navy pilot (in legend, at any rate) began shouting, "I've got a MiG at zero! A MiG at zero!"—meaning that it had maneuvered in behind him and was locked in on his tail. An irritated voice cut in and said, "Shut up and die like an aviator."

Tom Wolfe, *The Right Stuff*

What you definitely *don't* want to do is go out like a woman. If you're shot during some manly gang warfare, for instance, you don't want to expire like Richard Beymer at the end of *West Side Story,* lying in your girlfriend's arms and singing some dumb song about when you're going to meet again. How can you have any respect for a guy like that?

One final word: If you find it impossible, or at least terribly inconvenient, to make it to the electric chair or the scene of a gun fight, then it's an acceptable alternative to kick off by having a massive heart attack while engaged in sex with a voluptuous starlet. If you can't make them say, "He went out like a man," at least let them say, "What a way to go!"

MANLY EXTRA

Don't take the little woman for granted. Every now and then, let her know how much you appreciate her cooking.

HOW TO COMPORT YOURSELF AT YOUR FUNERAL

Once you've bought the farm in the proper manner, there is only one thing left for you to do: pay strict attention to the rules of manly comportment at your funeral. Here, of course, you have far less control over events, so it's important to prepare for things well in advance of the big day.

One point to bear in mind is that, if you're opting for the open coffin look, make sure that nobody puts any makeup on your face. If you're man enough to die, your friends and relatives should be man enough to pay respects to you in your naturally rugged (if somewhat anemic) state.

Also of great importance is to select your pallbearers with great care. A good rule of thumb is never to let your coffin be carried by anyone to whom you wouldn't have been proud to lend your car.

Finally, don't tolerate any floral arrangements at your funeral. Just because you're dead doesn't mean you want to be treated like some kind of fruit. You may notice when you're dead that people have a tendency to forget that they're dealing with a man. So it's up to you to play the part of a man right up until the moment they start shovelling the soil on the roof of your cozy, new knotty pine bachelor's pad. Stay hard. Keep a stiff upper lip. Never complain, never explain. Other than that, the main thing is just to relax and have a good time. After all—you've earned it.

WHAT'S WRONG WITH THIS PICTURE?

PHOTO QUIZ #6

It is vital to pick your pallbearers with care. Although the deceased in this picture obviously took great pains to choose men of sterling character to bear his coffin to its final resting place, they seem to be committing a terrible *faux pas*. What is it they're doing wrong?

Answer: Two of the pallbearers are carrying flowers! No man wants to have flowers at his funeral. The only possible excuse for this seemingly incomprehensible lapse in judgement is that these flowers were actually sent by some misguided female mourner, and the devoted pallbearers have removed them from the funeral parlor with the intention of tossing them into the first garbage can they pass on their way to the gravesite.

FINAL EXAM

All right, so you've read and digested every page of this book. So you know everything there is to know about being a man and you're finally ready to make your way in the world in the properly manly manner. Well, not so fast, trooper. There is one last hurdle before you: *The Manly Handbook* final exam.

The following questions are multiple-choice. Read them over carefully, then select the correct answer to each one. Now don't get nervous. Only your very fitness for life on this planet depends on how well you do on this test. Just answer the questions to the best of your ability and face the consequences. If you pull through all right, we'll be waiting for you on the other side, ready to join with you in restoring this country to its former manly greatness. We'll be looking for you. Good luck. All right now you men—get moving!

1. When your barber asks if you want a manicure, you should give him:
   a. a tip
   b. a funny look
   c. a flying headlock
   d. all of the above

2. What should your wife get you for Christmas?
   a. a book
   b. a tie
   c. an apron
   d. a Black-and-Decker chainsaw

3. When you overhear a guy in your local deli asking if he can have a taste of the brie cheese, you can be sure that he is:
   a. a crypto-Marxist
   b. a warped male impersonator who is a danger to the very fabric of our nation
   c. a foreigner
   d. all of the above

4. I read the books of Hermann Hesse:
   a. often
   b. every once in a while
   c. rarely
   d. Hey, c'mon, give me a break

5. If you are about to take the last seat on the bus and a really good-looking woman gets on behind you, you should:
   a. offer her the seat
   b. tell her to take a hike
   c. allow her to sit in your lap
   d. rip her dress off

6. If you come to a party and you see that they are serving quiche, you should:
   a. leave
   b. piss on the floor
   c. call the FBI
   d. either a, b, or c

7. What is the temperature range men most enjoy when they are outdoors?
   a. 55 to 60° F
   b. 70 to 75° F
   c. 80 to 85° F
   d. −10 to −5° F

8. When your girlfriend tells you she wants an open relationship, you should:
   a. cry
   b. agree
   c. tell her you'll pretend you never heard that
   d. start writing her telephone number on the walls of public toilets

9. How should you celebrate your son's high school graduation?
   a. punch him in the shoulder until he cries
   b. get your family together so you can all share the experience
   c. take him to a twi-night doubleheader
   d. a, then c

10. Which college should your son attend?
    a. Vassar
    b. Fashion Institute of Technology
    c. Wilfrid Academy of Hair and Beauty Culture
    d. Notre Dame

11. How should you spend New Year's Eve?
    a. In a quiet restaurant, having a candlelit dinner with the wife
    b. In Times Square, waiting for the ball to drop
    c. In Times Square, clearing Broadway with a night stick
    d. In the men's room of the Eagle Tavern, using the toilet seat as a pillow
    e. c and d

Essay Question: In fifteen words or less, answer the following question: Who was the greatest man who ever lived?

ANSWERS

1. c
2. d
3. d
4. d
5. c (a man is always polite)
6. d
7. d (provided you're wearing nothing heavier than a windbreaker)
8. c (a man is always merciful)
9. d
10. d
11. e

Essay question: If you've read this book all the way through and didn't immediately answer, "John Wayne, because he was an American and didn't take guff from Mexicans," then read it again.

SCORE

12... Mission accomplished
8–11... Job well done
4–7... There's still a chance. Restrict your TV watching to John Ford Westerns, read nothing except hard-boiled detective fiction and *Soldier of Fortune* magazine, and ask your doctor if he'll start you in on a treatment of male hormone shots.
0–3... See if you can get your money back from the bookstore, then use it to buy yourself a pair of pantyhose.

MAN
THE WAY
GOD MEANT
HIM TO BE

THE MANLY END